<u>Reading Shakespeare can be a real headache</u>

That's why we've put this book together.

We've put notes handily next to the play so you don't have to go hunting for "Note 136". That means you can understand what all the weird bits mean without losing the flow of the play.

We've written the notes in plain English to make it just that bit easier.

There's even the odd bit of ever-so-nearly entertaining humour in the notes and pictures to help you breeze through the toughest of scenes.

We've done our bit — the rest is up to you.

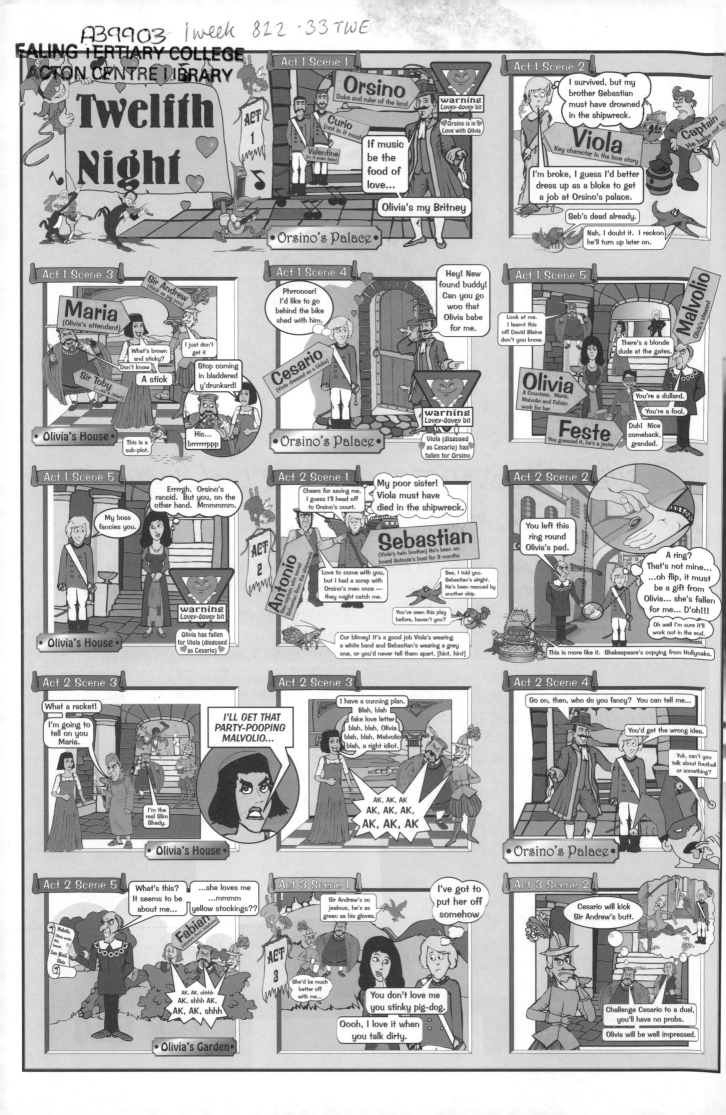

CONTENTS

Published by Coordination Group Publications, Ltd.

Editors:
Taissa Csáky
Tim Major
Becky May
Katherine Reed
Contributor:
William Shakespeare

ISBN: 1 84146 121 0
Groovy website: www.cgpbooks.co.uk
Jolly bits of clipart from CorelDRAW
Printed by Elanders Hindson, Newcastle upon Tyne.
Text, design, layout and original illustrations © Coordination Group Publications Ltd 2002

Orsino says how much he loves Olivia, but is told she is mourning her brother's death for seven years. Bad luck Orsino.

ACT 1 SCENE 1
Orsino's palace

Music. Enter ORSINO, *Duke of Illyria,* CURIO, *and other Lords*

ORSINO If music be the food of love, play on —
 Give me excess of it, that, surfeiting,
 The appetite may sicken, and so die.
 That strain again, it had a dying fall —
 O it came o'er my ear like the sweet sound   5
 That breathes upon a bank of violets,
 Stealing and giving odour. Enough — no more.
 'Tis not so sweet now as it was before.
 O spirit of love, how quick and fresh art thou,
 That, notwithstanding thy capacity,   10
 Receiveth as the sea. Nought enters there,
 Of what validity and pitch soe'er,
 But falls into abatement and low price
 Even in a minute. So full of shapes is fancy,
 That it alone is high fantastical.   15

CURIO Will you go hunt, my lord?

ORSINO   What, Curio?

CURIO The hart.

ORSINO Why so I do, the noblest that I have.
 O when mine eyes did see Olivia first,
 Methought she purged the air of pestilence; 20
 That instant was I turned into a hart,
 And my desires like fell and cruel hounds
 E'er since pursue me.

    Enter VALENTINE
   How now, what news from her?

VALENTINE So please my lord, I might not be admitted,
 But from her handmaid do return this answer: 25
 The element itself, till seven years' heat,
 Shall not behold her face at ample view —
 But like a cloistress she will veilèd walk,
 And water once a day her chamber round
 With eye-offending brine — all this to season 30
 A brother's dead love, which she would keep fresh
 And lasting, in her sad remembrance.

ORSINO O she that hath a heart of that fine frame
 To pay this debt of love but to a brother,
 How will she love, when the rich golden shaft 35
 Hath killed the flock of all affections else
 That live in her — when liver, brain, and heart,
 These sovereign thrones, are all supplied and filled
 Her sweet perfections with one selfsame king!
 Away before me to sweet beds of flowers — 40
 Love-thoughts lie rich when canopied with bowers.

    Exeunt

2-4 'Give me enough music to make my love so sick of it that it dies. Play that bit again — it was cool.'

7-8 'Stop it — it's not so good anymore.'

10-14 'Love is like the sea, devouring everything. Nothing can satisfy it.'

fancy = *love*

high fantastical = *really imaginative*

hart = *male deer*

19-23 'It was love at first sight. Since then thoughts of her have followed me everywhere.'

pestilence = *plague*

24-31 'They wouldn't let me in, but her maid (Maria) told me she won't show her face for seven years. She'll hide away like a nun and cry bitter tears for her brother.'

season = *preserve, keep alive*

rich golden shaft = *Cupid's arrow*

33-39 'If she can love a brother that much, think what she'll be like when she falls in love with me.'

liver, brains and heart: *the liver was supposed to be where passion came from. Thought came from the brain. Emotion came from the heart.*

bowers = *leafy, secluded places*

2

Viola's worried about her brother. The captain tells her about Orsino and Olivia. She decides to disguise herself as a man and serve Orsino.

ACT 1 SCENE 2
The sea-coast of Illyria

Enter VIOLA, *a* SEA CAPTAIN, *and Sailors*

VIOLA What country, friends, is this?

CAPTAIN This is Illyria, lady.

VIOLA And what should I do in Illyria?
My brother, he is in Elysium.
Perchance he is not drowned: what think you, sailors? 5

CAPTAIN It is perchance that you yourself were saved.

VIOLA O my poor brother! And so perchance may he be.

CAPTAIN True, madam, and to comfort you with chance,
Assure yourself, after our ship did split,
When you, and those poor number saved with you, 10
Hung on our driving boat, I saw your brother
Most provident in peril, bind himself
(Courage and hope both teaching him the practice)
To a strong mast that lived upon the sea —
Where like Arion on the dolphin's back 15
I saw him hold acquaintance with the waves
So long as I could see.

VIOLA For saying so, there's gold.
Mine own escape unfoldeth to my hope,
Whereto thy speech serves for authority, 20
The like of him. Know'st thou this country?

CAPTAIN Ay, madam, well, for I was bred and born
Not three hours' travel from this very place.

VIOLA Who governs here?

CAPTAIN A noble duke in nature as in name. 25

VIOLA What is his name?

CAPTAIN Orsino.

VIOLA Orsino! I have heard my father name him.
He was a bachelor then.

CAPTAIN And so is now, or was so very late; 30
For but a month ago I went from hence,
And then 'twas fresh in murmur (as you know
What great ones do, the less will prattle of)
That he did seek the love of fair Olivia.

VIOLA What's she? 35

CAPTAIN A virtuous maid, the daughter of a count
That died some twelvemonth since, then leaving her
In the protection of his son, her brother,
Who shortly also died — for whose dear love
(They say) she hath abjured the sight 40
And company of men.

VIOLA   O that I served that lady,
And might not be delivered to the world
Till I had made mine own occasion mellow
What my estate is!

CAPTAIN   That were hard to compass,
Because she will admit no kind of suit, 45

Side notes

4-5 'My brother's in heaven, unless he didn't drown.'

6 'It was only luck that saved you.'

provident = full of foresight

Arion = musician from ancient Greece saved from drowning by a dolphin.

19-21 'My own escape and what you have said give me hope that my brother is still alive.'

29 'He was single then.'

31-34 'When I left there was a rumour that Orsino was trying to marry Olivia.'

40-41 'She has sworn not to look at or mix with men.' abjured = rejected

41-44 'I wish I could work for her and hide away until I have decided what to do.'

44-46 'That'll be hard to bring about — she won't listen to anyone's requests, not even Orsino's.'

No, not the duke's.

VIOLA   There is a fair behaviour in thee, captain,
And though that nature with a beauteous wall
Doth oft close in pollution, yet of thee
I well believe thou hast a mind that suits   50
With this thy fair and outward character.
I prithee (and I'll pay thee bounteously)
Conceal me what I am, and be my aid
For such disguise as haply shall become
The form of my intent. I'll serve this duke.   55
Thou shalt present me as an eunuch to him —
It may be worth thy pains — for I can sing,
And speak to him in many sorts of music
That will allow me very worth his service.
What else may hap, to time I will commit,   60
Only shape thou thy silence to my wit.

CAPTAIN   Be you his eunuch, and your mute I'll be —
When my tongue blabs, then let mine eyes not see.

VIOLA   I thank thee. Lead me on.

Exeunt

47-55 'You appear to be good, but appearances can be deceptive. I trust you anyway. Help me disguise myself as a man.'

eunuch = castrated male servant

60-61 'I'll wait and see what happens, but for now don't tell anyone.'

hap = happen

63 'I'd go blind rather than spill the beans.'

ACT 1   SCENE 3
Olivia's house

Enter SIR TOBY *and* MARIA

Maria complains about Sir Toby's drunkenness and says Sir Andrew is foolish. Sir Andrew proves it, and boasts of his dancing skills.

SIR TOBY   What a plague means my niece to take the death of
her brother thus? I am sure care's an enemy to life.

1-2 'Olivia's mourning spoils all our fun.'

MARIA   By my troth, Sir Toby, you must come in earlier o' nights.
Your cousin, my lady, takes great exceptions to your ill hours.

4 'Olivia doesn't like you coming in late at night.'

SIR TOBY   Why, let her except, before excepted.   5

5 'She can object if she likes.'

MARIA   Ay, but you must confine yourself within the modest
limits of order.

6-7 'But you've got to control yourself.'

SIR TOBY   Confine? I'll confine myself no finer than I am: these
clothes are good enough to drink in, and so be these boots
too — and they be not, let them hang themselves in their own   10
straps.

MARIA   That quaffing and drinking will undo you: I heard my
lady talk of it yesterday and of a foolish knight that you
brought in one night here to be her wooer.

12 'Your drunkenness will be your downfall.'

SIR TOBY   Who, Sir Andrew Aguecheek?   15

MARIA   Ay, he.

SIR TOBY   He's as tall a man as any's in Illyria.

tall = brave

MARIA   What's that to th' purpose?

SIR TOBY   Why, he has three thousand ducats a year.

MARIA   Ay, but he'll have but a year in all these ducats. He's a   20
very fool and a prodigal.

20 'All that money will only last him a year.'

ducats = money

SIR TOBY   Fie, that you'll say so! He plays o' th'
viol-de-gamboys, and speaks three or four languages word
for word without book, and hath all the good gifts of nature.

viol-de-gamboys = musical instrument

23-24 'He's learnt 3 or 4 languages — by copying, not from books.'

MARIA   He hath indeed all, most natural — for besides that he's   25

25-29 'He's a simpleton, and an argumentative fool. If he wasn't such a coward, he would've been killed yonks ago.'

a fool, he's a great quarreller — and but that he hath the gift of a coward to allay the gust he hath in quarrelling, 'tis thought among the prudent he would quickly have the gift of a grave.

SIR TOBY   By this hand, they are scoundrels and substractors that say so of him. Who are they?   30

32-33 'They also say he gets drunk every night with you.'

MARIA   They that add, moreover, he's drunk nightly in your company.

34-37 'But only through drinking toasts to Olivia. Anyone who wouldn't drink to her until their head spins like a whipping top is a worthless coward.'

SIR TOBY   With drinking healths to my niece! I'll drink to her as long as there is a passage in my throat and drink in Illyria —   35
he's a coward and a coistrill that will not drink to my niece till his brains turn o' th' toe like a parish top. What, wench! *Castiliano vulgo* : for here comes Sir Andrew Agueface.

Castiliano vulgo = straight faces

Enter SIR ANDREW

SIR ANDREW   Sir Toby Belch! How now, Sir Toby Belch?

SIR TOBY   Sweet Sir Andrew!   40

ATI... SHOO!   A Fair Shrew

shrew = mouse or bad-tempered woman

SIR ANDREW   Bless you, fair shrew.

MARIA   And you too, sir.

SIR TOBY   Accost, Sir Andrew, accost.

accost = pay her a compliment

SIR ANDREW   What's that?

chambermaid = personal servant

SIR TOBY   My niece's chambermaid.   45

SIR ANDREW   Good Mistress Accost, I desire better acquaintance.

MARIA   My name is Mary, sir.

SIR ANDREW   Good Mistress Mary Accost –

50-51 Sir Toby keeps going on about 'accosting' here. He's making lots of saucy gags about flirting with Maria.

SIR TOBY   You mistake, knight. 'Accost' is front her, board her,   50
woo her, assail her.

SIR ANDREW   By my troth, I would not undertake her in this company. Is that the meaning of 'accost'?

fare you well = goodbye, farewell

MARIA   Fare you well, gentlemen.

SIR TOBY   And thou let part so, Sir Andrew, would thou mightst   55
never draw sword again.

←Fools

SIR ANDREW   And you part so, mistress, I would I might never draw sword again. Fair lady, do you think you have fools in hand?

in hand = to deal with

MARIA   Sir, I have not you by th' hand.   60

marry = by the Virgin Mary!

SIR ANDREW   Marry, but you shall have, and here's my hand.

buttery-bar = a ledge for tankards

MARIA   Now, sir, thought is free. I pray you bring your hand to th' buttery-bar and let it drink.

wherefore = why

SIR ANDREW   Wherefore, sweetheart? What's your metaphor?

dry = empty, stupid

MARIA   It's dry, sir.   65

SIR ANDREW   Why, I think so. I am not such an ass but I can keep my hand dry. But what's your jest?

MARIA   A dry jest, sir.

SIR ANDREW   Are you full of them?

at my fingers' ends = at my fingertips

I am barren = I've got no ideas

MARIA   Ay, sir, I have them at my fingers' ends — marry,   70
now I let go your hand, I am barren.

Exit

SIR TOBY O knight, thou lack'st a cup of canary.

canary = sweet wine from Canary Islands

Hands him a cup

When did I see thee so put down?

SIR ANDREW Never in your life, I think, unless you see canary
put me down. Methinks sometimes I have no more wit than   75
a Christian or an ordinary man has, but I am a great eater of
beef, and I believe that does harm to my wit.

75-77 'Sometimes I think I might not be that bright. Maybe it's because I eat too much beef.'

SIR TOBY No question.

SIR ANDREW And I thought that, I'd forswear it. I'll ride home
tomorrow, Sir Toby.   80

SIR TOBY *Pourquoi,* my dear knight?

pourquoi = why

SIR ANDREW What is *'pourquoi'*? Do, or not do? I would I
had bestowed that time in the tongues that I have in fencing,
dancing, and bear-baiting. O had I but followed the arts!

82-84 'I wish I'd spent less time having fun and more time learning intellectual stuff' Sir Toby makes a pun about 'tongues' (languages) and 'tongs' (hair curling tongs) to confuse Sir Andrew.

SIR TOBY Then hadst thou had an excellent head of hair.   85

SIR ANDREW Why, would that have mended my hair?

SIR TOBY Past question, for thou seest it will not curl by nature.

SIR ANDREW But it becomes me well enough, does't not?

88 'It suits me well enough, doesn't it?'

SIR TOBY Excellent — it hangs like flax on a distaff; and I hope
to see a housewife take thee between her legs and spin it off.   90

flax on a distaff = linen on a spindle for making thread

SIR ANDREW Faith, I'll home tomorrow, Sir Toby — your niece
will not be seen, or if she be, it's four to one, she'll none of
me. The count himself here hard by woos her.

91-93 'By heck, I'll go home tomorrow. Olivia's not seeing anyone and certainly not me. Orsino's trying to woo her too.'

SIR TOBY She'll none o' th' count; she'll not match above her
degree, neither in estate, years, nor wit. I have heard her   95
swear't. Tut, there's life in't, man.

94-96 'She won't marry anyone with a higher title, or older or cleverer than her — so you're still in with a chance, mate.'

SIR ANDREW I'll stay a month longer. I am a fellow o' th'
strangest mind i' th' world — I delight in masques and revels
sometimes altogether.

masques = fancy dress parties

revels = celebrations

SIR TOBY Art thou good at these kickshawses, knight?   100

kickshawses = silly things

SIR ANDREW As any man in Illyria, whatsoever he be, under
the degree of my betters, and yet I will not compare with an
old man.

SIR TOBY What is thy excellence in a galliard, knight?

SIR ANDREW Faith, I can cut a caper.   105

SIR TOBY And I can cut the mutton to't.

105 'By God, I can jump.'

caper = jump, also a spice eaten with mutton

SIR ANDREW And I think I have the back-trick simply as strong
as any man in Illyria.

SIR TOBY Wherefore are these things hid? Wherefore have
these gifts a curtain before 'em? Are they like to take dust,   110
like Mistress Mall's picture? Why dost thou not go to church
in a galliard and come home in a coranto? My very walk
should be a jig — I would not so much as make water but in
a sink-a-pace. What dost thou mean? Is it a world to hide
virtues in? I did think, by the excellent constitution of thy leg,   115
it was formed under the star of a galliard.

109-110 'Why do you keep your skill at dancing hidden?' Sir Toby is trying to persuade Sir Andrew to start dancing.

galliard, coranto, jig, and sink-a-pace are all types of dance

115-116 'Looking at your legs, I'd say you were born for dancing.'

SIR ANDREW Ay, 'tis strong, and it does indifferent well in a dun-
coloured stock. Shall we set about some revels?

117-118 'Yep, my leg's strong, and it looks ace in a brown stocking. Let's party.'

SIR TOBY What shall we do else? Were we not born under
Taurus?   120

121 *Each star sign was thought to control a different part of the body.*

SIR ANDREW Taurus? That's sides and heart.

SIR TOBY No, sir, it is legs and thighs. Let me see thee caper. Ha, higher! Ha, ha, excellent!

Exeunt

Duke Orsino tells Viola (who's pretending to be a man) to win Olivia for him. Viola's miffed because she fancies Orsino herself.

ACT 1 SCENE 4
Orsino's palace

Enter VALENTINE, *and* VIOLA *in man's attire.*

attire = *clothes*

VALENTINE If the duke continue these favours towards you, Cesario, you are like to be much advanced. He hath known you but three days, and already you are no stranger.

1-3 *'If Orsino carries on like this, you're bound to be promoted. He's only known you 3 days, and he thinks you're the tops.'*

VIOLA You either fear his humour or my negligence, that you call in question the continuance of his love. Is he inconstant, 5
sir, in his favours?

4 *'You're either scared of his moodiness or my carelessness.'*

5-6 *'Does he always blow hot and cold?'*

VALENTINE No, believe me.

VIOLA I thank you. Here comes the count.

Enter DUKE ORSINO, CURIO, *and Attendants*

ORSINO Who saw Cesario, ho?

VIOLA On your attendance, my lord — here. 10

aloof = *apart*

ORSINO *(To Curio and the Attendants)*
Stand you a while aloof, *(To Viola)* Cesario,
Thou know'st no less but all — I have unclasped
To thee the book even of my secret soul.
Therefore, good youth, address thy gait unto her;
Be not denied access, stand at her doors, 15
And tell them, there thy fixèd foot shall grow
Till thou have audience.

12-17 *'I've told you all my secrets. So go and stand outside Olivia's house and don't leave until you see her.'*

address thy gait = *direct your steps*

VIOLA   Sure, my noble lord,
If she be so abandoned to her sorrow
As it is spoke, she never will admit me.

17-19 *'But if she's as sad as people say she is, she'll never let me in.'*

ORSINO Be clamorous and leap all civil bounds, 20
Rather than make unprofited return.

20-21 *'Be noisy and impolite, rather than come away empty-handed.'*

VIOLA Say I do speak with her, my lord, what then?

23-27 *'Tell her how much I love her and need her. It'll sound better coming from someone young.'*

ORSINO O then, unfold the passion of my love,
Surprise her with discourse of my dear faith;
It shall become thee well to act my woes: 25
She will attend it better in thy youth
Than in a nuncio's of more grave aspect.

discourse = *stories, talk*

nuncio = *messenger*

grave aspect = *serious appearance*

VIOLA I think not so, my lord.

29-34 *'They'll not notice that you're an adult. You've got lovely red lips and a weedy voice, as if you were a woman. I know you're the man for the job.'*

ORSINO   Dear lad, believe it —
For they shall yet belie thy happy years,
That say thou art a man — Diana's lip 30
Is not more smooth and rubious — thy small pipe
Is as the maiden's organ, shrill and sound,
And all is semblative a woman's part.
I know thy constellation is right apt
For this affair. Some four or five attend him; 35
All, if you will — for I myself am best

Diana = *goddess of the moon (and love)*

rubious = *red*

constellation = *destiny*

When least in company. Prosper well in this,
And thou shalt live as freely as thy lord,
To call his fortunes thine.

VIOLA   I'll do my best
To woo your lady. (*Aside*) Yet, a barful strife!   40
Whoe'er I woo, myself would be his wife.

Exeunt

ACT 1 SCENE 5
Olivia's house

Enter MARIA *and* FESTE

MARIA Nay, either tell me where thou hast been, or I will not open my lips so wide as a bristle may enter in way of thy excuse. My lady will hang thee for thy absence.

FESTE Let her hang me: he that is well hanged in this world needs to fear no colours.   5

MARIA Make that good.

FESTE He shall see none to fear.

MARIA A good lenten answer. I can tell thee where that saying was born, of 'I fear no colours.'

FESTE Where, good Mistress Mary?   10

MARIA In the wars; and that may you be bold to say in your foolery.

FESTE Well, God give them wisdom that have it; and those that are fools, let them use their talents.

MARIA Yet you will be hanged for being so long absent — or to   15
be turned away: is not that as good as a hanging to you?

FESTE Many a good hanging prevents a bad marriage; and for turning away, let summer bear it out.

MARIA You are resolute then?

FESTE Not so neither, but I am resolved on two points –   20

MARIA That if one break, the other will hold, or if both break, your gaskins fall.

FESTE Apt, in good faith, very apt. Well, go thy way — if Sir Toby would leave drinking, thou wert as witty a piece of Eve's flesh as any in Illyria.   25

MARIA Peace, you rogue, no more o' that. Here comes my lady — make your excuse wisely, you were best.

Exit

FESTE Wit, and't be thy will, put me into good fooling! Those wits that think they have thee do very oft prove fools, and I that am sure I lack thee may pass for a wise man. For what says   30
Quinapalus? 'Better a witty fool than a foolish wit'.

Enter OLIVIA *and Attendants, with* MALVOLIO

God bless thee, lady.

OLIVIA Take the fool away.

FESTE Do you not hear, fellows? Take away the lady.

OLIVIA Go to, y'are a dry fool: I'll no more of you — besides,   35

Side notes:

37-39 'If you do well then I'll make you rich.'

40-41 'What a pickle! I'd rather marry Orsino myself.'

Feste comes to ask Olivia to take him on as her Fool again. Malvolio tries to put her off. Viola/Cesario comes with a message from Orsino — but Olivia's more interested in the messenger.

1-3 'You're in real trouble. Where have you been?'

4-5 'If you're dead you've got nothing to be scared of.'

6 'Explain that.'

7 'He won't see anything to be afraid of.'

lenten answer = a weak joke

13-14 'My fooling is a God-given gift, so let me use it.'

15-16 'You'll be hanged or sacked by Olivia for being away so long.'

points = laces to hold gaskins up

gaskins = trousers

23-25 'If only Sir Toby would stop drinking, you'd be the best wife for him in Illyria.'

27 'You'd better make your excuse wisely.'

Quinapalus = name Feste makes up — he's pretending to be clever

35-36 'Come off it, you've run out of jokes. I don't want anything more to do with you. Besides, you're getting unreliable.'

dry = empty

you grow dishonest.

FESTE Two faults, madonna, that drink and good counsel will
amend: for give the dry fool drink, then is the fool not dry
— bid the dishonest man mend himself — if he mend, he is
no longer dishonest; if he cannot, let the botcher mend him. 40
Anything that's mended is but patched: virtue that
transgresses is but patched with sin, and sin that amends is
but patched with virtue. If that this simple syllogism will
serve, so — if it will not, what remedy? As there is no true
cuckold but calamity, so beauty's a flower. The lady bade 45
take away the fool — therefore I say again, take her away.

OLIVIA Sir, I bade them take away you.

FESTE Misprision in the highest degree! Lady, *cucullus non facit
monachum* — that's as much to say as I wear not motley in
my brain. Good madonna, give me leave to prove you a fool. 50

OLIVIA Can you do it?

FESTE Dexteriously, good madonna.

OLIVIA Make your proof.

FESTE I must catechise you for it, madonna. Good my mouse
of virtue, answer me. 55

OLIVIA Well, sir, for want of other idleness, I'll bide your proof.

FESTE Good madonna, why mourn'st thou?

OLIVIA Good fool, for my brother's death.

FESTE I think his soul is in hell, madonna.

OLIVIA I know his soul is in heaven, fool. 60

FESTE The more fool, madonna, to mourn for your brother's
soul being in heaven. Take away the fool, gentlemen.

OLIVIA What think you of this fool, Malvolio? Doth he not
mend?

MALVOLIO Yes, and shall do, till the pangs of death shake him: 65
infirmity, that decays the wise, doth ever make the better fool.

FESTE God send you, sir, a speedy infirmity, for the better
increasing your folly! Sir Toby will be sworn that I am no
fox, but he will not pass his word for twopence that you are
no fool. 70

OLIVIA How say you to that, Malvolio?

MALVOLIO I marvel your ladyship takes delight in such a
barren rascal. I saw him put down the other day with an
ordinary fool that has no more brain than a stone. Look you
now, he's out of his guard already. Unless you laugh and 75
minister occasion to him, he is gagged. I protest I take these
wise men that crow so at these set kind of fools no better
than the fools' zanies.

OLIVIA O you are sick of self-love, Malvolio, and taste with a
distempered appetite. To be generous, guiltless, and of free 80
disposition is to take those things for bird-bolts that you deem
cannon bullets. There is no slander in an allowed fool though
he do nothing but rail; nor no railing in a known discreet
man though he do nothing but reprove.

FESTE Now Mercury endue thee with leasing, for thou speak'st 85

Marginal notes:

37-38 'A drink and good advice will fix those two faults.'
39-40 'Tell the dishonest man to mend himself — if he mends he's not dishonest anymore. If he can't improve he'll have to be patched.'
transgresses = goes wrong
bade = ordered syllogism = formula
cuckold = someone whose partner has been unfaithful
cucullus non facit monachum = you're not a monk just because you wear the outfit
49-50 'I may wear fool's clothes, but inside I'm no fool.'
dexteriously = brilliantly
catechise = ask you questions
56 'As I have nothing better to do, I wait for you to prove it.'

63-64 'Isn't he improving?'
65-66 'He'll get better till he dies. The more feeble he gets the better he'll be at fooling.'
68-70 'Toby wouldn't say I'm clever, but even if you paid him he wouldn't deny you're a fool.'
72-74 'I'm amazed you find him funny. I saw him the other day with a completely brainless fool.'
out of his guard = lost his concentration
minister occasion = fuss over
76-78 'Wise people who laugh at this sort of fool are no better than the fools.'
79-80 'Malvolio, you're so pompous. You take things too seriously.'
81-82 'make mountains out of molehills'
82-84 'He's not insulting you, even when he's ranting — nor does a wise man rant, even when he's criticising.'
Mercury = god of liars

well of fools!

Enter MARIA

85-86 'Let Mercury teach you to lie, as you speak kindly of fools.'

MARIA   Madam, there is at the gate a young gentleman much desires to speak with you.

OLIVIA   From the Count Orsino, is it?

MARIA   I know not, madam — 'tis a fair young man and well attended.   90

well attended = *with lots of servants*

OLIVIA   Who of my people hold him in delay?

MARIA   Sir Toby, madam, your kinsman.

OLIVIA   Fetch him off, I pray you — he speaks nothing but madman. Fie on him.   95

madman = *madman's talk*

Exit MARIA

Go you, Malvolio. If it be a suit from the count, I am sick, or not at home — what you will to dismiss it.

96-97 'If he's come with a message of love from Orsino, make an excuse and send him away.'

Exit MALVOLIO

Now you see, sir, how your fooling grows old, and people dislike it.

FESTE   Thou hast spoke for us, madonna, as if thy eldest son should be a fool: whose skull Jove cram with brains, for — here he comes —   100

100-101 'You stood up for me so well that you'd make a good mother for a fool.'

103 'one of your relatives is a bit soft in the head.'

Enter SIR TOBY *(staggering)*

one of thy kin has a most weak *pia mater.*

pia mater = *brain*

OLIVIA   By mine honour, half drunk! What is he at the gate, cousin?   105

SIR TOBY   A gentleman.

OLIVIA   A gentleman! What gentleman?

SIR TOBY   'Tis a gentleman here — *(Hiccuping)* a plague o' these pickle herring! How now, sot?

FESTE   Good Sir Toby —   110

sot = *drunken fool*

OLIVIA   Cousin, cousin, how have you come so early by this lethargy?

lethargy = *sleepiness*

SIR TOBY   Lechery! I defy lechery. There's one at the gate.

OLIVIA   Ay, marry, what is he?

SIR TOBY   Let him be the devil and he will, I care not: give me faith, say I. Well, it's all one.   115

115-116 Don't worry — this doesn't make any sense. It's drunken ranting.

Exit

OLIVIA   What's a drunken man like, fool?

FESTE   Like a drowned man, a fool, and a madman — one draught above heat makes him a fool, the second mads him, and a third drowns him.   120

one draught above heat = *one drink over the limit*

OLIVIA   Go thou and seek the crowner, and let him sit o' my coz, for he's in the third degree of drink — he's drowned. Go look after him.

121-122 'Go and get the coroner, to do an inquest on my cousin — he's drunk so much he's drowned.'

FESTE   He is but mad yet, madonna, and the fool shall look to the madman.   125

124-125 'He's not drowned yet, just mad. I'll look after him.'

Exit

Enter MALVOLIO

MALVOLIO Madam, yond young fellow swears he will speak with you. I told him you were sick — he takes on him to understand so much and therefore comes to speak with you. I told him you were asleep — he seems to have a foreknowledge of that too, and therefore comes to speak with 130 you. What is to be said to him, lady? He's fortified against any denial.

have a foreknowledge = *know already*

131-132 *'Whatever I say he's got an excuse ready.'*

OLIVIA Tell him he shall not speak with me.

MALVOLIO H'as been told so — and he says he'll stand at your door like a sheriff's post, and be the supporter to a bench, 135 but he'll speak with you.

134-136 *'He's not going anywhere, until he's allowed to speak to you.'*

sheriff's post = *post that shows where the sheriff lives*

OLIVIA What kind o' man is he?

MALVOLIO Why, of mankind.

OLIVIA What manner of man?

MALVOLIO Of very ill manner. He'll speak with you, will you 140 or no.

140-141 *'He'll speak to you whether you like it or not.'*

OLIVIA Of what personage and years is he?

142 *'What does he look like and how old is he?'*

MALVOLIO Not yet old enough for a man, nor young enough for a boy: as a squash is before 'tis a peascod, or a codling when 'tis almost an apple. 'Tis with him in standing water, 145 between boy and man. He is very well-favoured and he speaks very shrewishly. One would think his mother's milk were scarce out of him.

squash = *unripe pea pod*

codling = *unripe apple*

146-148 *'He's handsome and speaks in a high-pitched voice. You'd think he'd barely stopped breast-feeding.'*

OLIVIA Let him approach. Call in my gentlewoman.

MALVOLIO Gentlewoman, my lady calls. 150

Exit

Enter MARIA

OLIVIA Give me my veil — come throw it o'er my face. We'll once more hear Orsino's embassy.

embassy = *ambassador, messenger*

Enter VIOLA

VIOLA The honourable lady of the house, which is she?

OLIVIA Speak to me, I shall answer for her. Your will?

VIOLA Most radiant, exquisite, and unmatchable beauty — I 155 pray you tell me if this be the lady of the house, for I never saw her. I would be loath to cast away my speech: for besides that it is excellently well penned, I have taken great pains to con it. Good beauties, let me sustain no scorn — I am very comptible, even to the least sinister usage. 160

157-160 *'I wouldn't want to waste my speech — it's well written and I've learnt it by heart. Don't make fun of me — I'm very sensitive.'*

comptible = *sensitive*

sinister usage = *rough treatment*

OLIVIA Whence came you, sir?

161 *'Where are you from?'*

VIOLA I can say little more than I have studied, and that question's out of my part. Good gentle one, give me modest assurance if you be the lady of the house, that I may proceed in my speech. 165

162-164 *'I have learned what I am going to say, and that's not part of it. Please give me at least some reassurance that you really are Olivia.'*

OLIVIA Are you a comedian?

166 *'Are you an actor?'*

VIOLA No, my profound heart — and yet, by the very fangs of malice, I swear, I am not that I play. Are you the lady of the house?

167-168 *'No, honestly not — though I admit I'm not quite who I seem.'*

OLIVIA If I do not usurp myself, I am. 170

170 *'Yes, unless I'm pretending to be me.'*

VIOLA   Most certain, if you are she, you do usurp yourself: for what is yours to bestow is not yours to reserve. But this is from my commission. I will on with my speech in your praise, and then show you the heart of my message.

171-173 'You are betraying yourself — your love might be your own but you've no right to keep it to yourself. But anyway, that wasn't in my instructions.'

OLIVIA   Come to what is important in't: I forgive you the praise.   175

175 'I'll let you off the praise.'

VIOLA   Alas, I took great pains to study it, and 'tis poetical.

OLIVIA   It is the more like to be feigned — I pray you keep it in. I heard you were saucy at my gates, and allowed your approach rather to wonder at you than to hear you. If you be mad, be gone; if you have reason, be brief. 'Tis not that   180 time of moon with me to make one in so skipping a dialogue.

177 'It's likely to be false.'
178-179 'I only let you in to look at you, because I heard you were being cheeky at the gates.'
180-181 'I'm not feeling mad enough for this silly conversation.'

MARIA   Will you hoist sail, sir? Here lies your way.

VIOLA   No, good swabber, I am to hull here a little longer. Some mollification for your giant, sweet lady! Tell me your mind, I am a messenger.   185

hoist sail = leave
swabber = deck-scrubber
to hull = stay

OLIVIA   Sure you have some hideous matter to deliver, when the courtesy of it is so fearful. Speak your office.

186-187 'You must have some terrible message to be so polite.'

VIOLA   It alone concerns your ear. I bring no overture of war, no taxation of homage — I hold the olive in my hand — my words are as full of peace as matter.   190

188-189 'I'm not here to warn you of a quarrel, or to order you to be obedient.'
189-190 'There's as much peace in my words as there is business.'

OLIVIA   Yet you began rudely. What are you? What would you?

VIOLA   The rudeness that hath appeared in me I learned from my entertainment. What I am, and what I would, are as secret as maidenhead: to your ears, divinity — to any other's,   195 profanation.

193-195 'I was rude in reaction to my treatment. What I am and want are as secret as virginity.'
profanation = blasphemy

OLIVIA   Give us the place alone — we will hear this divinity.
                    Exeunt MARIA *and* ATTENDANTS
Now, sir, what is your text?

VIOLA   Most sweet lady –

OLIVIA   A comfortable doctrine, and much may be said of it.   200 Where lies your text?

VIOLA   In Orsino's bosom.

OLIVIA   In his bosom? In what chapter of his bosom?

VIOLA   To answer by the method, in the first of his heart.

OLIVIA   O! I have read it. It is heresy. Have you no more to   205 say?

by the method = in the same style
heresy = lies

VIOLA   Good madam, let me see your face.

OLIVIA   Have you any commission from your lord to negotiate with my face? You are now out of your text, but we will draw the curtain and show you the picture.   210
                    Unveiling
Look you, sir, such a one I was this present. Is't not well done?

208-212 'Did Orsino ask you to talk to my face? You've changed the subject, but I'll show you my face. Look, it's a recent portrait. Isn't it well painted?'

VIOLA   Excellently done, if God did all.

OLIVIA   'Tis in grain, sir; 'twill endure wind and weather.

214 'The colour won't run.'

VIOLA   'Tis beauty truly blent, whose red and white   215 Nature's own sweet and cunning hand laid on. Lady, you are the cruellest she alive, If you will lead these graces to the grave,

blent = blended
217-219 'You're the cruellest woman alive if you die without leaving the world children, as a record of your beauty.'

12

Jumble Sale — everything 50p

227 'even if you were the devil I'd have to admit you're beautiful.'

228-230 'Even if you were so beautiful that no one else's beauty came close to yours, it would only be fair repayment for Orsino's love.'

nonpareil = unequalled

234-238 'I assume he's virtuous, know he's noble, wealthy, young, has a good reputation, is generous, educated, brave, and handsome. But I can't love him.'

240-242 'If I loved you as passionately and painfully as Orsino, I wouldn't see the logic in your refusal.'

willow = symbol of unhappy love

246 'write faithful poems about my rejected love'

248 'shout your name in praise to the echoing hills'

babbling gossip = echo

250-252 'You would find no rest in this world until you took pity on me.'

253 'What sort of people were your parents?'

Nah, keep your purse. It doesn't even go with my outfit.

254 'Better off than I am now, but I'm doing OK'

259 Olivia tries to give Cesario money.

fee'd post = paid messenger

262-264 'When you do fall in love, I hope his heart will be like flint so that your passion is ignored like my master's.'

And leave the world no copy.

OLIVIA   O sir, I will not be so hard-hearted. I will give out divers   220
schedules of my beauty. It shall be inventoried and every
particle and utensil labelled to my will, as, *item,* two lips,
indifferent red; *item,* two grey eyes, with lids to them; *item,*
one neck, one chin, and so forth. Were you sent hither to
praise me?   225

VIOLA   I see you what you are. You are too proud —
But if you were the devil, you are fair!
My lord and master loves you. O such love
Could be but recompensed, though you were crowned
The nonpareil of beauty.

OLIVIA   How does he love me?   230

VIOLA   With adorations, fertile tears,
With groans that thunder love, with sighs of fire.

OLIVIA   Your lord does know my mind. I cannot love him.
Yet I suppose him virtuous, know him noble,
Of great estate, of fresh and stainless youth;   235
In voices well divulged, free, learned, and valiant,
And in dimension, and the shape of nature,
A gracious person. But yet I cannot love him.
He might have took his answer long ago.

VIOLA   If I did love you in my master's flame,   240
With such a suffering, such a deadly life,
In your denial I would find no sense;
I would not understand it.

OLIVIA   Why, what would you?

VIOLA   Make me a willow cabin at your gate,
And call upon my soul within the house —   245
Write loyal cantons of contemnèd love,
And sing them loud even in the dead of night —
Hallow your name to the reverberate hills,
And make the babbling gossip of the air
Cry out 'Olivia!' O you should not rest   250
Between the elements of air and earth
But you should pity me!

OLIVIA   You might do much.
What is your parentage?

VIOLA   Above my fortunes, yet my state is well:
I am a gentleman.

OLIVIA   Get you to your lord.   255
I cannot love him. Let him send no more —
Unless (perchance) you come to me again,
To tell me how he takes it. Fare you well.
I thank you for your pains. Spend this for me.

VIOLA   I am no fee'd post, lady — keep your purse,   260
My master, not myself, lacks recompense.
Love make his heart of flint that you shall love,
And let your fervour like my master's be
Placed in contempt. Farewell, fair cruelty.

Exit

Act 1, Scene 5

OLIVIA 'What is your parentage?'   265
   'Above my fortunes, yet my state is well:
   I am a gentleman.' I'll be sworn thou art —
   Thy tongue, thy face, thy limbs, actions, and spirit
   Do give thee five-fold blazon. Not too fast! Soft, soft!
   Unless the master were the man — How now?   270
   Even so quickly may one catch the plague?
   Methinks I feel this youth's perfections
   With an invisible and subtle stealth
   To creep in at mine eyes. Well, let it be.
   What ho, Malvolio!

Enter MALVOLIO

MALVOLIO   Here, madam, at your service.   275

OLIVIA Run after that same peevish messenger,
   The county's man. He left this ring behind him,
   Would I, or not. Tell him, I'll none of it.
   Desire him not to flatter with his lord,
   Nor hold him up with hopes — I am not for him.   280
   If that the youth will come this way tomorrow,
   I'll give him reasons for't. Hie thee, Malvolio!

MALVOLIO Madam, I will.

Exit

OLIVIA I do I know not what, and fear to find
   Mine eye too great a flatterer for my mind.   285
   Fate, show thy force; ourselves we do not owe.
   What is decreed must be — and be this so.

Exit

265-267 Olivia repeats what Cesario said — she's smitten with him.

five-fold blazon = a five part coat of arms

This wasn't meant to happen...

270-274 'Now if the boss was this chap — hang on, can you really fall in love so fast? I think I'm falling for him.'

276-277 'Run after that irritating messenger, Count Orsino's man.'

to flatter with = encourage

284-285 'I don't know what I'm doing. I'm afraid my eyes might be misleading my mind.'

owe = own

287 'What fate decrees must happen — so let this happen.'

Act 1, Scene 5

Revision Summary — Act 1

These questions are about the <u>whole</u> of Act 1. Some of them are in really picky detail — because that's exactly the kind of detail you have to go into in your essays. You have to know all about why Shakespeare used the language that he did, as well as being clued up with the plot of the play. Keep practising these questions until you can answer them without looking at the play.

1) In which country does Twelfth Night take place?

2) Write out Orsino's speech about Olivia in lines 19-23 of Scene 1 in your own words.

3) How does Curio try to distract Orsino in Scene 1?

4) What does Orsino mean when he talks about the liver, brain and heart in lines 37-39 of Scene 1? Is it about:
   a) his medical problems,   b) the places where emotions are held in the body
   or   c) his lunch?

5) In Scene 1, what reason does Valentine give for Olivia being sad and avoiding men?

6) Why is Viola upset when she arrives on shore after being shipwrecked?

7) What does "abjured" mean (Scene 2, line 40)?

8) In Act 1 Viola decides to disguise herself as a "eunuch" — what is that?

9) What does Maria warn Sir Toby about in Scene 3?

10) What do Sir Toby and Maria think of Sir Andrew? Quote three phrases to back up your answer.

11) What does "accost" mean?

12) Explain the pun about 'tongues' and 'tongs' in lines 82-90 of Scene 3.

13) What does Viola call herself when she's in disguise?

14) What does Viola think of Orsino? Quote one phrase from Act 1 to back up your answer.

15) What is Feste's profession?

16) What reasons does Olivia give for being sick of Feste in Scene 5?

17) Write out everything that Olivia and Feste say in lines 35-46 of Scene 5 in your own words.

18) Explain how Feste proves his argument that Olivia is a fool in Scene 5.

19) Write out Olivia's speech about Malvolio and Feste in lines 79-84 of Scene 5 in your own words.

20) Write down three phrases or sentences from Scene 5 that show that Malvolio doesn't like Feste.

21) Who arrives at the gates to Olivia's house in Scene 5?

22) Why is Olivia annoyed with Sir Toby in Scene 5?

23) What does Olivia compare her face to, when she lifts her veil?

24) Quote three phrases that Viola uses to tell Olivia that she is beautiful.

25) Write out Viola's speech in lines 239-251 of Scene 5 in your own words.

26) Write down a sentence or phrase from Scene 5 that shows that Olivia fancies Viola when she's dressed as a man.

27) Who is described as 'the county's man'?

28) What does Olivia ask Malvolio to do at the end of Act 1?

29) Write out Olivia's speech at lines 283-286 of Scene 5 in your own words.

ACT 2 SCENE 1
The sea-coast of Illyria
Enter ANTONIO *and* SEBASTIAN

> Viola's brother, Sebastian, has been saved from the shipwreck by Antonio. He thinks Viola is dead. He decides to leave Antonio and go to Orsino's court. Antonio says he has enemies in Orsino's court but then follows him anyway.

ANTONIO Will you stay no longer? Nor will you not that I go with you?

SEBASTIAN By your patience, no. My stars shine darkly over me: the malignancy of my fate might perhaps distemper yours — therefore I shall crave of you your leave that I may bear my evils alone. It were a bad recompense for your love, to lay any of them on you. 5

ANTONIO Let me yet know of you whither you are bound.

SEBASTIAN No, sooth, sir: my determinate voyage is mere extravagancy. But I perceive in you so excellent a touch of modesty, that you will not extort from me what I am willing to keep in — therefore it charges me in manners the rather to express myself. You must know of me then, Antonio, my name is Sebastian, which I called Roderigo. My father was that Sebastian of Messaline, whom I know you have heard of. He left behind him myself and a sister, both born in an hour: if the heavens had been pleased, would we had so ended! But you, sir, altered that, for some hour before you took me from the breach of the sea was my sister drowned. 10 ... 15

ANTONIO Alas the day! 20

SEBASTIAN A lady, sir, though it was said she much resembled me, was yet of many accounted beautiful: but, though I could not with such estimable wonder overfar believe that, yet thus far I will boldly publish her — she bore a mind that envy could not but call fair. She is drowned already, sir, with salt water, though I seem to drown her remembrance again with more. 25

ANTONIO Pardon me, sir, your bad entertainment.

SEBASTIAN O good Antonio, forgive me your trouble.

ANTONIO If you will not murder me for my love, let me be your servant. 30

SEBASTIAN If you will not undo what you have done, that is, kill him whom you have recovered, desire it not. Fare ye well at once — my bosom is full of kindness, and I am yet so near the manners of my mother, that upon the least occasion more mine eyes will tell tales of me. I am bound to the Count Orsino's court. Farewell. 35

Exit

ANTONIO The gentleness of all the gods go with thee!
I have many enemies in Orsino's court,
Else would I very shortly see thee there.
But, come what may, I do adore thee so,
That danger shall seem sport, and I will go. 40

Exit

3-7 'Don't stay in my company — I'm having a run of bad luck.'
malignancy = evil influence
distemper = infect
whither = where
sooth = indeed
9-10 'No, indeed, sir — I've got no fixed plans of where I'll travel.'
10-13 'You're so nice you deserve some explanation of who I am.'
16-19 'My sister was born at the same time as me and it almost looked as if we'd die at the same time, too — but she was drowned and I was saved.'
breach = breaking waves
with such estimable wonder = in all modesty
21-27 'People said my sister was beautiful — but she looked like me so I'm not sure that's possible. She was clever though. I've drowned the memory of her in tears.'
entertainment = welcome
your trouble = all this bother
30-31 'Let me be your servant — I like you so much, losing you would kill me.'
recovered = rescued
32-37 Don't ask me to kill you unless you want me (the man you saved) to die too. I'm so like my mother that I'll probably cry. I'm going to Orsino's court.'
39-42 'I shouldn't go to Orsino's court because I have enemies there. But I care about Sebastian, so I'll go anyway.'
sport = fun

Malvolio catches up with Viola, who has just left Olivia. He tries to give her a ring and says Olivia isn't interested in Orsino. Viola is confused because she didn't give Olivia a ring. She realises Olivia fancies her.

ACT 2 SCENE 2
A street
Enter VIOLA, MALVOLIO *following*

1 *'Did you just visit Olivia?'* ⟶ MALVOLIO Were not you even now with the Countess Olivia?

2-3 *'Yes, I've only just got here.'* ⟶ VIOLA Even now, sir, on a moderate pace, I have since arrived but hither.

5-9 *'She said to tell Orsino that she isn't interested in him, and not to return unless it's to say he's got the ring back.'* ⟶ MALVOLIO She returns this ring to you, sir — you might have saved me my pains, to have taken it away yourself. She adds, 5 moreover, that you should put your lord into a desperate assurance she will none of him. And one thing more, that you be never so hardy to come again in his affairs, unless it be to report your lord's taking of this. Receive it so.

desperate assurance = absolutely no doubt

10 *'I'm not taking the ring back.'* ⟶ VIOLA She took the ring of me. I'll none of it. 10

peevishly = irritably

MALVOLIO Come, sir, you peevishly threw it to her — and her will is, it should be so returned. If it be worth stooping for, there it lies, in your eye — if not, be it his that finds it.

12-13 *'If it's worth getting down on your hands and knees to get it, have it.'*

Exit

14-19 *'I didn't give her a ring, why did she make that up? Crikey, Olivia is in love with me! She was completely tongue-tied.'* ⟶ VIOLA I left no ring with her: what means this lady?
Fortune forbid my outside have not charmed her! 15
She made good view of me — indeed, so much,
That methought her eyes had lost her tongue,
For she did speak in starts distractedly.
She loves me, sure — the cunning of her passion

churlish messenger = rude messenger (Malvolio)

Invites me in this churlish messenger. 20
None of my lord's ring? Why, he sent her none.
I am the man; if it be so, as 'tis,
Poor lady, she were better love a dream.

24-25 *'The disguise I'm wearing is a source of evil — the devil is at work.'* ⟶ Disguise, I see, thou art a wickedness,

pregnant enemy = the devil

proper-false = good-looking men

Wherein the pregnant enemy does much. 25
How easy is it for the proper-false

waxen = changeable/fickle

In women's waxen hearts to set their forms!
Alas, our frailty is the cause, not we,
For such as we are made of, such we be.

26-27 *'It's so easy for women to become smitten with good-looking men.'*

How will this fadge? My master loves her dearly, 30
And I, poor monster, fond as much on him;
And she, mistaken, seems to dote on me.

fadge = turn out

dote on = be infatuated with

What will become of this? As I am man,
My state is desperate for my master's love,

30-38 *'Orsino likes Olivia, I like Orsino and Olivia likes me. This is far too complicated for me to fix. I'll let time sort it out.'* ⟶ As I am woman — now alas the day! — 35
What thriftless sighs shall poor Olivia breathe?
O time! Thou must untangle this, not I;
It is too hard a knot for me to untie.

thriftless = wasted

Exit

Sir Toby, Sir Andrew and Feste get very drunk one night and make a lot of noise. Maria tries to shush them. Malvolio walks in and is really angry about the noise. Maria hatches a plan for them to get their own back on Malvolio.

ACT 2 SCENE 3
Olivia's house
Enter SIR TOBY *and* SIR ANDREW

1-2 *'not to be in bed after midnight is to be up early'* ⟶ SIR TOBY Approach, Sir Andrew — not to be abed after midnight is to be up betimes; and *diluculo surgere*, thou

diluculo surgere = rising at dawn is healthy (Latin)

know'st —

SIR ANDREW   Nay, by my troth, I know not: but I know, to be
up late is to be up late.   5

SIR TOBY   A false conclusion: I hate it as an unfilled can.
To be up after midnight and to go to bed then, is
early: so that to go to bed after midnight is to go to bed
betimes. Does not our life consist of the four elements?

SIR ANDREW   Faith, so they say — but I think it rather consists   10
of eating and drinking.

SIR TOBY   Thou'rt a scholar; let us therefore eat and drink.
Marian, I say! A stoup of wine!

Enter FESTE

SIR ANDREW   Here comes the fool, i' faith.

FESTE   How now, my hearts? Did you never see the picture of   15
'We Three'?

SIR TOBY   Welcome, ass. Now let's have a catch.

SIR ANDREW   By my troth, the fool has an excellent breast.
I had rather than forty shillings I had such a leg, and so sweet
a breath to sing, as the fool has. In sooth, thou wast in very   20
gracious fooling last night, when thou spokest of
Pigrogromitus, of the Vapians passing the equinoctial of
Queubus. 'Twas very good, i' faith: I sent thee sixpence for
thy leman: hadst it?

FESTE   I did impeticos thy gratillity; for Malvolio's nose is no   25
whipstock: my lady has a white hand, and the Myrmidons
are no bottle-ale houses.

SIR ANDREW   Excellent! Why, this is the best fooling, when all
is done. Now, a song.

SIR TOBY   Come on, there is sixpence for you. Let's have a   30
song.

SIR ANDREW   There's a testril of me too: if one knight give a —

FESTE   Would you have a love song, or a song of good life?

SIR TOBY   A love song, a love song.

SIR ANDREW   Ay, ay. I care not for good life.   35

FESTE   *(Sings)*
O mistress mine, where are you roaming?
O, stay and hear, your true love's coming,
That can sing both high and low.
Trip no further, pretty sweeting:
Journeys end in lovers meeting,   40
Every wise man's son doth know.

SIR ANDREW   Excellent good, i' faith.

SIR TOBY   Good, good.

FESTE   *(Sings)*
What is love? 'Tis not hereafter;
Present mirth hath present laughter;   45
What's to come is still unsure.
In delay there lies no plenty,
Then come kiss me, sweet and twenty;
Youth's a stuff will not endure.

by my troth = *I swear*

unfilled can = *empty tankard*

four elements = *earth, wind, water and fire*

thou'rt = *you are*

stoup = *jug*

'We Three' = *a picture of two fools, making the person looking at the picture the third fool.*

catch = *song sung as a round*

breast = *singing voice*

19-20 *'I'd give forty shillings to be able to sing like Feste.'*

Pigrogromitus, Vapians, Queubus = *made-up names*

23-24 *'I sent you sixpence for your sweetheart — did you get it?'*
25-27 *Feste is talking nonsense.*

whipstock = *whip handle*

Myrmidons = *soldiers of Achilles, a famous Greek warrior*

testril = *sixpence*

song of good life = *drinking song*

The song is about love and enjoying yourself while you can.

39 *'Walk no further, pretty darling'*

Every wise man's son... there's a saying that wise men have fools for sons

47 *'Waiting won't get you anywhere.'*

49 *'You won't be young forever.'*

mellifluous = *sweet*

contagious = *infectious, unpleasant (implies bad breath)*

52 *'Yes, sweet and infectious.'* ⟶

welkin = *sky*

53-56 *'It would be a sweet unpleasantness to hear through your nose. Shall we get even more rowdy and sing really loudly?'* ⟶

dog = *expert*

catch = *song*

constrained = *ordered*

They agree to sing a song as a round where the chorus is 'Hold thy peace, thou knave'. The joke is that they're yelling 'be quiet' very loudly.

SHUT UP!
SHUT UP!
SHUT UP!

66-68 *'What a noise! If Olivia hasn't asked Malvolio to chuck you out yet, I might do it.'* ⟶

Peg-a-Ramsey = *a dance, it might mean a spoilsport here*

consanguineous = *related by blood (to his niece Olivia)*

beshrew = *curse*

75-77 *Sir Andrew makes himself sound like an idiot by saying he is a "natural" at playing the fool.* ⟶

78 *The line of the song might be a reference to the title of 'Twelfth Night'.* ⟶

80-84 *'What are you doing making so much noise at this time of night? You're treating Olivia's house like it was a pub.'* ⟶

coziers catches = *shoemakers' songs*

mitigation or remorse = *shame*

Sneck up! = *Be hanged!*

round = *blunt*

88-93 *'Olivia says, even though you're her relation, that if you don't start behaving yourself she'll want you to go.'* ⟶

SIR ANDREW A mellifluous voice, as I am true knight. 50

SIR TOBY A contagious breath.

SIR ANDREW Very sweet and contagious, i' faith.

SIR TOBY To hear by the nose, it is dulcet in contagion. But shall we make the welkin dance indeed? Shall we rouse the night-owl in a catch that will draw three souls out of one 55 weaver? Shall we do that?

SIR ANDREW And you love me, let's do't: I am dog at a catch.

FESTE By'r lady, sir, and some dogs will catch well.

SIR ANDREW Most certain. Let our catch be, 'Thou knave.'

FESTE 'Hold thy peace, thou knave,' knight? I shall be 60 constrained in't to call thee knave, knight.

SIR ANDREW 'Tis not the first time I have constrained one to call me knave. Begin, fool. It begins, 'Hold thy peace.'

FESTE I shall never begin if I hold my peace.

SIR ANDREW Good, i' faith. Come, begin. 65

Catch sung

Enter MARIA

MARIA What a caterwauling do you keep here! If my lady have not called up her steward Malvolio and bid him turn you out of doors, never trust me.

SIR TOBY My lady's a Cataian, we are politicians, Malvolio's a Peg-a-Ramsey, and (*Sings*) Three merry men be we. 70 Am not I consanguineous? Am I not of her blood? Tilly-vally! 'Lady!' (*Sings*) There dwelt a man in Babylon, lady, lady!

FESTE Beshrew me, the knight's in admirable fooling.

SIR ANDREW Ay, he does well enough if he be disposed, and 75 so do I too — he does it with a better grace, but I do it more natural.

SIR TOBY (*Sings*) O, the twelfth day of December —

MARIA For the love o' God, peace!

Enter MALVOLIO

MALVOLIO My masters, are you mad? Or what are you? Have 80 ye no wit, manners, nor honesty, but to gabble like tinkers at this time of night? Do ye make an alehouse of my lady's house, that ye squeak out your coziers' catches without any mitigation or remorse of voice? Is there no respect of place, persons, nor time in you? 85

SIR TOBY We did keep time, sir, in our catches.
Sneck up!

MALVOLIO Sir Toby, I must be round with you. My lady bade me tell you that, though she harbours you as her kinsman, she's nothing allied to your disorders. If you can separate 90 yourself and your misdemeanors, you are welcome to the house — if not, and it would please you to take leave of her, she is very willing to bid you farewell.

SIR TOBY (*Sings*) Farewell, dear heart, since I must needs be gone. 95

MARIA Nay, good Sir Toby.

FESTE (*Sings*) His eyes do show his days are almost done.

MALVOLIO Is't even so?

SIR TOBY (*Sings*) But I will never die.

FESTE (*Sings*) Sir Toby, there you lie.   100

MALVOLIO This is much credit to you.

SIR TOBY (*Sings*) Shall I bid him go?

FESTE (*Sings*) What and if you do?

SIR TOBY (*Sings*) 'Shall I bid him go, and spare not?'

FESTE (*Sings*) O no, no, no, no, you dare not.   105

SIR TOBY Out o' tune, sir? Ye lie! Art any more than a
  steward? Dost thou think, because thou art virtuous, there
  shall be no more cakes and ale?

FESTE Yes, by Saint Anne, and ginger shall be hot i' the mouth
  too.   110

Exit

SIR TOBY Thou'rt i' the right. Go, sir, rub your chain with
  crumbs. A stoup of wine, Maria!

MALVOLIO Mistress Mary, if you prized my lady's favour at
  anything more than contempt, you would not give means
  for this uncivil rule — she shall know of it, by this hand.   115

Exit

MARIA Go shake your ears.

SIR ANDREW 'Twere as good a deed as to drink when a man's
  a-hungry, to challenge him the field, and then to break
  promise with him and make a fool of him.

SIR TOBY Do't, knight: I'll write thee a challenge; or I'll   120
  deliver thy indignation to him by word of mouth.

MARIA Sweet Sir Toby, be patient for tonight. Since the youth
  of the Count's was today with thy lady, she is much out of
  quiet. For Monsieur Malvolio, let me alone with him. If I do
  not gull him into a nayword, and make him a common   125
  recreation, do not think I have wit enough to lie straight in
  my bed: I know I can do it.

SIR TOBY Possess us, possess us, tell us something of
  him.

MARIA Marry, sir, sometimes he is a kind of puritan.   130

SIR ANDREW O, if I thought that I'd beat him like a dog!

SIR TOBY What, for being a puritan? Thy exquisite
  reason, dear knight?

SIR ANDREW I have no exquisite reason for't, but I have
  reason good enough.   135

MARIA The devil a puritan that he is, or anything constantly,
  but a time-pleaser, an affectioned ass, that cons state
  without book and utters it by great swarths. The best
  persuaded of himself, so crammed (as he thinks) with
  excellencies, that it is his grounds of faith that all that look on   140
  him love him — and on that vice in him will my revenge find
  notable cause to work.

98, 101 Malvolio is furious but can't do much to stop them fooling around. He resorts to sarcastic comments.

106-108 'You're only a steward. Do you think no-one should have a good time just because of you?'

108 Cakes and ale were associated with parties and frowned on by strict Christians.

109 Ginger was used to spice ale.

111-112 'clean your steward's chain.' Sir Toby's being offensive about the fact that Malvolio's a servant.

113-115 'Maria, if you respected Olivia you wouldn't provide drinks for this party. I'm going to tell on you.'

go shake your ears = an insult

117-119 'It's as funny as drinking on an empty stomach to challenge someone to a duel and then bail out and leave them looking a fool.'

122-127 'Calm down. Olivia's been in a state ever since meeting Orsino's boy (Cesario). If you give me time I'll trick Malvolio into looking a complete idiot. I'm clever enough.'

gull = trick

nayword = fool

possess us = tell us

puritan = religious and austere

exquisite = excellent

136-142 'Malvolio learns fancy expressions by heart and then parrots them. He is vain and thinks everyone loves him. I can use that weakness to trick him.'

Act 2, Scene 3

144-147 'I'll drop a letter in Malvolio's path. It'll be a fake love letter from Olivia to Malvolio. I won't mention his name but describe him so he can't help but recognise himself.'

gait = walk

expressure = expression

device = trick

Sir Andrew keeps repeating what Sir Toby has just said. He does this a lot.

a horse of that colour = in that vein

sport royal = great fun

physic = medicine

159-161 'My plan will work. I'll hide you and the fool near where I drop the letter to see his reaction.'

Penthesilea = Queen of the Amazons

beagle = small hunting dog

167 Sir Andrew seems quite sad here, which is quite touching and makes a change from him acting a twit.

168-169 Sir Toby wants Sir Andrew to get more money so he can sponge off him.

170-171 'If Olivia doesn't marry me, I'm in a mess because of the time and money I've wasted.'

cut = fool

burn some sack = warm and spice some sherry

175-176 Sir Toby refers back to his lines at the beginning of the scene.

SIR TOBY   What wilt thou do?

MARIA   I will drop in his way some obscure epistles of love, wherein, by the colour of his beard, the shape of his leg, the manner of his gait, the expressure of his eye, forehead, and complexion, he shall find himself most feelingly personated. I can write very like my lady your niece: on a forgotten matter we can hardly make distinction of our hands.   145

SIR TOBY   Excellent, I smell a device.   150

SIR ANDREW   I have't in my nose too.

SIR TOBY   He shall think, by the letters that thou wilt drop, that they come from my niece, and that she's in love with him.

MARIA   My purpose is indeed a horse of that colour.   155

SIR ANDREW   And your horse now would make him an ass.

MARIA   Ass, I doubt not.

SIR ANDREW   O, 'twill be admirable!

MARIA   Sport royal, I warrant you — I know my physic will work with him. I will plant you two, and let the fool make a third, where he shall find the letter — observe his construction of it. For this night, to bed, and dream on the event. Farewell.   160

Exit

SIR TOBY   Good night, Penthesilea.

SIR ANDREW   Before me, she's a good wench.

SIR TOBY   She's a beagle, true-bred, and one that adores me: what o' that?   165

SIR ANDREW   I was adored once too.

SIR TOBY   Let's to bed, knight. Thou hadst need send for more money.

SIR ANDREW   If I cannot recover your niece, I am a foul way out.   170

SIR TOBY   Send for money, knight — if thou hast her not i' the end, call me cut.

SIR ANDREW   If I do not, never trust me, take it how you will.

SIR TOBY   Come, come, I'll go burn some sack — 'tis too late to go to bed now. Come, knight; come, knight.   175

Exeunt

Feste sings Orsino a song. Then Viola and Orsino discuss love. Orsino thinks only men can feel love strongly, but Viola argues women can too.

ACT 2   SCENE 4
Orsino's palace

Enter ORSINO, VIOLA, CURIO, *and others*

ORSINO   Give me some music.

Musicians step forward

Now, good morrow, friends.
Now, good Cesario, but that piece of song,
That old and antic song we heard last night:
Methought it did relieve my passion much,
More than light airs and recollected terms   5

2-5 'The song we heard last night made me feel a lot better.' Orsino is feeling love-sick for Olivia.

antic = quaint

light airs = easy-listening music

recollected terms = artificial words

Of these most brisk and giddy-paced times:
Come, but one verse.

CURIO   He is not here, so please your lordship that should sing it.

ORSINO   Who was it?

CURIO   Feste, the jester, my lord — a fool that the lady Olivia's   10
father took much delight in. He is about the house.

ORSINO   Seek him out, and play the tune the while.

Exit CURIO. *Music plays.*

Come hither, boy. If ever thou shalt love,
In the sweet pangs of it remember me:
For such as I am, all true lovers are,   15
Unstaid and skittish in all motions else,
Save in the constant image of the creature
That is beloved. How dost thou like this tune?

VIOLA   It gives a very echo to the seat
Where love is throned.

ORSINO   Thou dost speak masterly.   20
My life upon't, young though thou art, thine eye
Hath stayed upon some favour that it loves.
Hath it not, boy?

VIOLA   A little, by your favour.

ORSINO   What kind of woman is't?

VIOLA   Of your complexion.

ORSINO   She is not worth thee, then. What years, i' faith?   25

VIOLA   About your years, my lord.

ORSINO   Too old by heaven! Let still the woman take
An elder than herself — so wears she to him,
So sways she level in her husband's heart:
For, boy, however we do praise ourselves,   30
Our fancies are more giddy and unfirm,
More longing, wavering, sooner lost and worn,
Than women's are.

VIOLA   I think it well, my lord.

ORSINO   Then let thy love be younger than thyself,
Or thy affection cannot hold the bent: 35
For women are as roses, whose fair flower
Being once displayed, doth fall that very hour.

VIOLA   And so they are. Alas, that they are so:
To die, even when they to perfection grow!

Re-enter CURIO *and* FESTE

ORSINO   O, fellow, come, the song we had last night.   40
Mark it, Cesario, it is old and plain —
The spinsters and the knitters in the sun,
And the free maids that weave their thread with bones
Do use to chant it: it is silly sooth,
And dallies with the innocence of love,   45
Like the old age.

FESTE   Are you ready, sir?

ORSINO   Ay, prithee, sing.

---

giddy-paced = *hectic*

7 *'Come on, just one verse.'*

8 *'The bloke who sang it isn't here.'*

hither = *here*

13-18 *'If you ever fall in love think about how I am now. I'm like all true lovers — I'm unpredictable and playful in all my emotions, except my constant love for Olivia.'*
19-20 *'This music is just like love.'*

20-22 *'You're right. Although you're young you must have been in love once.'*

i'faith = *honestly*
24, 26 *Viola (who is in love with Orsino) says that the woman she was in love with had his complexion and was about his age.*

27-28 *Orsino says women should marry men older than themselves.*

sways she level = *stays the same*
31-33 *'Men's love is more impulsive and fickle, more intensive and changeable than women's.'*
worn = *worn out*

hold the bent = *stand the strain*

36-37 *'Women lose their beauty very quickly.'*

38 *'You're right, it's a shame.'*

42-44 *'The old maids and the carefree young girls sing that song.'*
silly sooth = *simple truth*
dallies = *plays*

22

cypress, yew = trees associated with death and churchyards

The song is about a man who dies of heartbreak and doesn't want to be remembered.

69 Orsino isn't in the mood for Feste's fooling and politely dismisses him.

melancholy god = Saturn, the planet believed to rule sad people

changeable taffeta = cloth which changes colour in the light.

72-75 Feste's implying that Orsino changes his mind a lot and links his moods to the unpredictability of the sea.

give place = leave us

sovereign cruelty = Olivia

77-80 'Go to Olivia and tell her I love her, and not because of her land and money.'

82-83 'It's her natural beauty that attracts me.'

pranks her in = adorns her with

85 'I won't take no for an answer.'

86-89 'What if a girl liked you, and you didn't love her? Wouldn't you want her to take no for an answer?'

90-93 'That wouldn't happen because women can't feel love as strongly as me.'

Music. Feste's song:

FESTE Come away, come away, death,
And in sad cypress let me be laid.   50
Fly away, fly away breath,
I am slain by a fair cruel maid:
      My shroud of white, stuck all with yew,
         O, prepare it.
      My part of death, no one so true   55
         Did share it.
Not a flower, not a flower sweet,
On my black coffin let there be strewn;
Not a friend, not a friend greet
My poor corpse, where my bones shall be thrown: 60
      A thousand thousand sighs to save,
         Lay me, O where
      Sad true lover never find my grave,
         To weep there.

ORSINO There's for thy pains.   65

Gives him money

FESTE No pains, sir, I take pleasure in singing, sir.

ORSINO I'll pay thy pleasure then.

FESTE Truly, sir, and pleasure will be paid, one time or another.

ORSINO Give me now leave to leave thee.

FESTE Now, the melancholy god protect thee, and the tailor   70
make thy doublet of changeable taffeta, for thy mind is a
very opal. I would have men of such constancy put to sea,
that their business might be everything and their intent
everywhere, for that's it that always makes a good voyage
of nothing. Farewell.   75

Exit

ORSINO Let all the rest give place.

Exit CURIO and Attendants

                              Once more, Cesario,
Get thee to yond same sovereign cruelty.
Tell her my love, more noble than the world,
Prizes not quantity of dirty lands —
The parts that fortune hath bestowed upon her,   80
Tell her, I hold as giddily as fortune —
But 'tis that miracle and queen of gems
That nature pranks her in attracts my soul.

VIOLA But if she cannot love you, sir?

ORSINO I cannot be so answered.

VIOLA   Sooth, but you must.   85
Say that some lady, as perhaps there is,
Hath for your love as great a pang of heart
As you have for Olivia: you cannot love her;
You tell her so — must she not then be answered?

ORSINO There is no woman's sides   90
Can bide the beating of so strong a passion
As love doth give my heart; no woman's heart
So big, to hold so much — they lack retention

Act 2, Scene 4

Alas, their love may be called appetite,
No motion of the liver, but the palate,   95
That suffers surfeit, cloyment and revolt;
But mine is all as hungry as the sea,
And can digest as much. Make no compare
Between that love a woman can bear me
And that I owe Olivia.

VIOLA   Ay, but I know —   100

ORSINO What dost thou know?

VIOLA Too well what love women to men may owe:
In faith, they are as true of heart as we.
My father had a daughter loved a man,
As it might be, perhaps, were I a woman,   105
I should your lordship.

ORSINO   And what's her history?

VIOLA A blank, my lord. She never told her love,
But let concealment, like a worm i' th' bud,
Feed on her damask cheek — she pined in thought,
And with a green and yellow melancholy   110
She sat like patience on a monument,
Smiling at grief. Was not this love indeed?
We men may say more, swear more, but indeed
Our shows are more than will — for still we prove
Much in our vows, but little in our love.   115

ORSINO But died thy sister of her love, my boy?

VIOLA I am all the daughters of my father's house,
And all the brothers too — and yet I know not.
Sir, shall I to this lady?

ORSINO   Ay, that's the theme.
To her in haste — give her this jewel, say   120
My love can give no place, bide no denay.

Exeunt

ACT 2 SCENE 5
Olivia's garden

Enter SIR TOBY, SIR ANDREW *and* FABIAN

SIR TOBY Come thy ways, Signior Fabian.

FABIAN Nay, I'll come. If I lose a scruple of this sport, let me be
boiled to death with melancholy.

SIR TOBY Wouldst thou not be glad to have the niggardly
rascally sheep-biter come by some notable shame?   5

FABIAN I would exult, man. You know he brought me out o'
favour with my lady about a bear-baiting here.

SIR TOBY To anger him, we'll have the bear again — and we will
fool him black and blue, shall we not, Sir Andrew?

SIR ANDREW And we do not, it is pity of our lives.   10

SIR TOBY Here comes the little villain.

Enter MARIA

Side annotations:

94-96 'Women's love is more like hunger. They don't have true feelings, and their taste suffers from over-eating, nausea and sickness.'

as hungry as the sea = referring to ship-wrecks

98-100 'Don't even try to compare women's love to the way I feel about Olivia.'

100 Viola butts in and almost gives herself away.

102-106 'Women can love as much as men can. My father had a daughter who loved a man as much as I might love you, if I were a woman.'

106 'What was her story?'

107-112 'Nothing happened — she kept her love a secret. She felt dreadful but bore it patiently.' (Viola is talking about herself.)

damask = pink

green and yellow melancholy = pale sadness

111 There are paintings from Shakespeare's time showing Patience as a person (sometimes on funeral monuments.)

114-115 'Men may talk a lot, but the strength of their feelings might not be that strong.'

117-118 Olivia talks in riddles about her being a woman.

theme = idea

bide no denay = accept no denial

Maria sets up the trick on Malvolio. Sir Toby, Fabian and Sir Andrew watch him fall for it.

1 'Hurry up, Fabian.'

2-3 'I'm coming. I'd rather die of sadness than miss this.'

4-5 'Wouldn't it be great to see that rotten Malvolio get seriously shown up?'

6-7 'I'd rejoice. You know he got me in trouble with Olivia about the bear fighting we had here.'

10 'If we didn't, we wouldn't deserve to live.'

SWAG

metal of India =
precious (literally gold)

13 'Everyone hide in the trees.'

14-17 'He's been practising his speech
for half an hour. Watch him — it'll be
hilarious — because I know this letter
will make a total fool of him.'

close = hide

19 Trout can be caught by
tickling their bellies till they float
back into the tickler's hands.

affect = admire

fancy = love

complexion = colouring

23-24 'Besides, she treats
me with more respect than
any of her other servants.'

26-27 'Be quiet! What a turkey!
Look at him strutting about with
his feathers puffed out!'

Bang!

'Slight = by God's light

32 'Shoot him!'

34-35 'If I married Olivia, I wouldn't
be the first servant to marry his Lady.'

fie = shame

Jezebel = shameless woman

blows him = puffs him up

state = throne

stone-bow = crossbow
that fires stones

branched = embroidered

day-bed = couch

47-49 'I would be very dignified.
I would look gravely at everyone, to
show I know my place, and they should
know theirs. Then I'd send for Toby.'

54 He nearly says 'my steward's
chain', then catches himself, and
says 'some rich jewel'.

How now, my metal of India?

MARIA Get ye all three into the box-tree. Malvolio's coming down this walk. He has been yonder i' the sun practising behaviour to his own shadow this half hour. Observe him, 15 for the love of mockery, for I know this letter will make a contemplative idiot of him. Close, in the name of jesting!

The men hide

Lie thou there —

Drops a letter

for here comes the trout that must be caught with tickling.

Exit

Enter MALVOLIO

MALVOLIO 'Tis but fortune — all is fortune. Maria once told me 20 she did affect me, and I have heard herself come thus near, that should she fancy, it should be one of my complexion. Besides, she uses me with a more exalted respect than any one else that follows her. What should I think on't?

SIR TOBY Here's an overweening rogue! 25

FABIAN O peace! Contemplation makes a rare turkey-cock of him — how he jets under his advanced plumes!

SIR ANDREW 'Slight, I could so beat the rogue!

FABIAN Peace, I say!

MALVOLIO To be Count Malvolio! 30

SIR TOBY Ah, rogue!

SIR ANDREW Pistol him, pistol him!

FABIAN Peace, peace!

MALVOLIO There is example for't. The Lady of the Strachy married the yeoman of the wardrobe — 35

SIR ANDREW Fie on him, Jezebel!

FABIAN O peace! Now he's deeply in. Look how imagination blows him.

MALVOLIO Having been three months married to her, sitting in my state — 40

SIR TOBY O for a stone-bow to hit him in the eye!

MALVOLIO Calling my officers about me, in my branched velvet gown, having come from a day-bed, where I have left Olivia sleeping —

SIR TOBY Fire and brimstone! 45

FABIAN O peace, peace!

MALVOLIO And then to have the humour of state; and after a demure travel of regard — telling them I know my place, as I would they should do theirs — to ask for my kinsman Toby —

SIR TOBY Bolts and shackles! 50

FABIAN O peace, peace, peace! Now, now!

MALVOLIO Seven of my people, with an obedient start, make out for him. I frown the while, and perchance wind up my watch, or play with my — some rich jewel. Toby approaches; curtsies there to me — 55

SIR TOBY   Shall this fellow live?

FABIAN   Though our silence be drawn from us by cars, yet
        peace!

MALVOLIO   I extend my hand to him thus, quenching my
        familiar smile with an austere regard of control —   60

SIR TOBY   And does not 'Toby' take you a blow o' the lips then?

MALVOLIO   Saying, 'Cousin Toby, my fortunes having cast me
        on your niece, give me this prerogative of speech —'

SIR TOBY   What, what?

MALVOLIO   'You must amend your drunkenness.'   65

SIR TOBY   Out, scab!

FABIAN   Nay, patience, or we break the sinews of our plot.

MALVOLIO   'Besides, you waste the treasure of your time with a
        foolish knight —'

SIR ANDREW   That's me, I warrant you.   70

MALVOLIO   'One Sir Andrew —'

SIR ANDREW   I knew 'twas I, for many do call me fool.

MALVOLIO

                        Taking up the letter
        What employment have we here?

SIR TOBY   Now is the woodcock near the gin.

FABIAN   O peace, and the spirit of humours intimate reading   75
        aloud to him!

MALVOLIO   By my life, this is my lady's hand: these be her very
        'C's, her 'U's, and her 'T's, and thus makes she her great 'P's.
        It is, in contempt of question, her hand.

SIR ANDREW   Her 'C's, her 'U's, and her 'T's — why that?   80

MALVOLIO   *(Reads)* 'To the unknown beloved, this, and my
        good wishes' — her very phrases! By your leave, wax. Soft!
        And the impressure her Lucrece, with which she uses to seal:
        'tis my lady. To whom should this be?

                        Opens the letter

FABIAN   This wins him, liver and all.   85

MALVOLIO   *(Reads)*   Jove knows I love,
                        But who?
                    Lips, do not move:
                        No man must know.'
        'No man must know.' What follows? The numbers altered!   90
        'No man must know'! If this should be thee, Malvolio!

SIR TOBY   Marry, hang thee, brock!

MALVOLIO   *(Reads)*   I may command where I adore,
                        But silence, like a Lucrece knife,
                    With bloodless stroke my heart doth gore;   95
                        M.O.A.I. doth sway my life.

FABIAN   A fustian riddle!

SIR TOBY   Excellent wench, say I.

MALVOLIO   'M.O.A.I. doth sway my life.' Nay, but first let me
        see, let me see — let me see.   100

---

cars = *horses and carts*

59-60 **'I shake his hand,
stopping myself from smiling my
usual smile with strict control.'**

62-63 **'Since I'm married to your
niece, I have the right to say this —'**

OUT SCAB!

break the sinews
    = *spoil*

warrant = *bet*

employment = *business*

74 **'Now the bird's near the trap.'**
Woodcocks were thought to be stupid.

75-76 **'Let's hope he reads it out loud.'**

77-79 **'It's definitely Olivia's handwriting.'**

82-84 **'This must be written by Olivia
— it sounds like her, and it has the
stamp she uses to seal her letters.'**
Lucrece = *woman who
    represents chastity.*

Jove = *Jupiter, Roman
    chief of the gods*

90 **'The metre changes!'**

brock = *badger*

Lucrece knife: *Lucrece stabbed
    herself after being raped.*

doth gore = *does wound*

sway = *rule*

fustian = *pretentious*

Not you! Him!

Gulp.

Act 2, Scene 5

Glossary / Paraphrase (left margin)	Text

dressed = prepared

102 *'And how quickly he's fallen for the trap.'*

staniel = kestrel

104-107 *'It's obvious to anyone of normal intelligence. There's nothing hard about this. But what does the arrangement of letters at the end mean?'*

109 *'He's lost the trail.'*

sowter = fox hound

rank = smelly

Yup - I'm sexy.

cur = dog

faults = cold scents

115-116 *'it doesn't make sense, and makes even less sense when you look closely'*

117 *'And the hangman's noose (O) will finish you off, I hope.'*

cudgel = beat with a club

120-121 *'If you had eyes in the back of your head you'd see you were losing more than you're looking forward to.'*

122-124 *'This doesn't look as hopeful for me as it did before, but you can __make__ it fit my name'*

125 *'If you get this letter, think carefully.'*

in my stars = by birth

128-133 *'Your fate is looking good. Embrace it body and soul. Practise for being what you're likely to become. Stop acting humbly. Antagonise a relative, be unfriendly to servants. Talk loudly about politics, get used to being noticed.'*

cross-gartered = with ribbons tied above and below the knee to hold up stockings

135-138 *'I tell you — your fortune's made if you want it. If not, just stick to being a steward, a companion of servants and unworthy of good fortune.'*

services = roles

141 *'This wouldn't be more obvious in broad daylight and open country.'*

politic = political

142-145 *'I'll put down Sir Toby, I'll stop mixing with uncivilised people. I will be, to every last detail, the man described in this letter. I won't be fooled — it's obvious she loves me.'*

manifests = declares

149-150 *'I'll stand apart and be proud'*

FABIAN   What dish o' poison has she dressed him!

SIR TOBY   And with what wing the staniel checks at it!

MALVOLIO   'I may command where I adore.' Why, she may command me: I serve her — she is my lady. Why, this is evident to any formal capacity. There is no obstruction in this, and the end — what should that alphabetical position portend? If I could make that resemble something in me — Softly! 'M.O.A.I.' — **105**

SIR TOBY   O ay, make up that! He is now at a cold scent.

FABIAN   Sowter will cry upon't for all this, though it be as rank as a fox. **110**

MALVOLIO   'M' — Malvolio. 'M' — why, that begins my name!

FABIAN   Did not I say he would work it out? The cur is excellent at faults.

MALVOLIO   'M' — but then there is no consonancy in the sequel; that suffers under probation. 'A' should follow, but 'O' does. **115**

FABIAN   And 'O' shall end, I hope.

SIR TOBY   Ay, or I'll cudgel him and make him cry 'O'!

MALVOLIO   And then 'I' comes behind.

FABIAN   Ay, and you had any eye behind you, you might see more detraction at your heels than fortunes before you. **120**

MALVOLIO   'M.O.A.I.' This simulation is not as the former, and yet, to crush this a little, it would bow to me, for every one of these letters are in my name. Soft, here follows prose. (Reads) 'If this fall into thy hand, revolve. In my stars I am above thee, but be not afraid of greatness. Some are born great, some achieve greatness, and some have greatness thrust upon 'em. Thy fates open their hands; let thy blood and spirit embrace them, and, to inure thyself to what thou art like to be, cast thy humble slough and appear fresh. Be opposite with a kinsman, surly with servants; let thy tongue tang arguments of state; put thy self into the trick of singularity. She thus advises thee that sighs for thee. Remember who commended thy yellow stockings and wished to see thee ever cross-gartered: I say, remember. Go to, thou art made if thou desir'st to be so — if not, let me see thee a steward still, the fellow of servants, and not worthy to touch Fortune's fingers. Farewell. She that would alter services with thee, **125** **130** **135**

                    The Fortunate-Unhappy.' **140**

Daylight and champain discovers not more! This is open. I will be proud, I will read politic authors, I will baffle Sir Toby, I will wash off gross acquaintance, I will be point-device, the very man. I do not now fool myself to let imagination jade me; for every reason excites to this, that my lady loves me. **145** She did commend my yellow stockings of late, she did praise my leg being cross-gartered — and in this she manifests herself to my love, and with a kind of injunction drives me to these habits of her liking. I thank my stars, I am happy. I will be strange, stout, in yellow stockings, and cross-gartered, even with the swiftness of putting on. Jove and my stars be praised! Here is yet a postscript. (Reads) 'Thou canst not **150**

choose but know who I am. If thou entertain'st my love, let
it appear in thy smiling; thy smiles become thee well.
Therefore in my presence still smile, dear my sweet, I prithee.' 155
Jove, I thank thee. I will smile — I will do everything that thou
wilt have me.

Exit

FABIAN   I will not give my part of this sport for a pension of
thousands to be paid from the Sophy.

SIR TOBY   I could marry this wench for this device —   160

SIR ANDREW   So could I, too.

SIR TOBY   And ask no other dowry with her but such another
jest.

SIR ANDREW   Nor I neither.

FABIAN   Here comes my noble gull-catcher.   165

Enter MARIA

SIR TOBY   Wilt thou set thy foot o' my neck?

SIR ANDREW   Or o' mine either?

SIR TOBY   Shall I play my freedom at tray-trip and become thy
bond-slave?

SIR ANDREW   I' faith, or I either?   170

SIR TOBY   Why, thou hast put him in such a dream that when
the image of it leaves him, he must run mad.

MARIA   Nay, but say true, does it work upon him?

SIR TOBY   Like aqua-vitae with a midwife.

MARIA   If you will then see the fruits of the sport, mark his first 175
approach before my lady. He will come to her in yellow
stockings, and 'tis a colour she abhors, and cross-gartered, a
fashion she detests — and he will smile upon her, which will
now be so unsuitable to her disposition, being addicted to a
melancholy as she is, that it cannot but turn him into a   180
notable contempt. If you will see it, follow me.

SIR TOBY   To the gates of Tartar, thou most excellent devil of wit!

SIR ANDREW   I'll make one too.

Exeunt

153-154 'If you are glad of my love, smile when you're with me — your smiles suit you.'

156-157 'I'll do everything you want me to'

161 For the rest of this scene Sir Andrew just echoes whatever Toby says.

Sophy = ruler of Persia

device = trick

dowry = marriage gift

gull-catcher = catcher of fools

168-169 'Shall I gamble my freedom and become your slave?'

aqua-vitae = alcoholic spirit

abhors = can't stand

178-181 'He'll smile at her, but she's so used to sadness now, that she'll think he's a disgrace.'

182 'To the gates of hell, you fiend.'

Revision Summary — Act 2

Don't skip on past — there's loads of important info in Act 2 that you need to learn. Do the questions below, and go back over them until you can remember the answers. That way you'll have a load of details about the play stored up in your brain when you come to write your essay.

1) What does Sebastian mean when he says, "My stars shine darkly over me," in Scene 1?

2) What good reason does Antonio have for not going to Orsino's court?

3) Which emotion does Antonio say he feels for Sebastian:
   a) love,   b) pity,   or c) jealousy?

4) What does Malvolio try to give to Viola in Scene 2? Who sent it?

5) Is anyone else on stage when Viola makes her speech, Scene 2 lines 14-38?

6) What does Viola think that Olivia's feelings are towards her?

7) Rewrite, in your own words, Sir Toby's line, "Not to be abed after midnight is to be up betimes" (Scene 3, lines 1-2).

8) What is a picture of "We Three"?

9) Why does Sir Toby give Feste sixpence?

10) What is the theme of the song in Scene 3, lines 36-49.

11) What is the repeated line of the song Feste, Sir Andrew and Sir Toby start to sing?

12) Which two characters walk in on the party? Who comes in first?

13) Write down three of the questions Malvolio asks, when telling off Sir Toby and his friends (Scene 3, lines 80-85)?

14) Write down Malvolio's message from Olivia to Sir Toby in your own words?

15) Who is the "youth of the Count's" Maria mentions in Scene 3, lines 122-123?

16) What character flaws does Maria say Malvolio has?

17) Describe Maria's plan to trick Malvolio.

18) What does Sir Toby want Sir Andrew to send for more of?

19) What does Sir Andrew say his situation will be if Olivia turns him down?

20) Who is Orsino love-sick for in Scene 4?

21) Orsino describes his love for Olivia as:
   a) hopeless — she'll never love him back,   b) perfect — a template for true love, or c) a passing infatuation?

22) Feste sings a song in Scene 4 — what is it about?

23) How does Orsino describe the love of women in Scene 4, lines 90-100? How does that compare with his comment in Scene 4, lines 31-33?

24) Viola describes a daughter of her father's, who loved a man but never told him. Who is she talking about?

25) What reason does Fabian have for disliking Malvolio (Scene 5, lines 6-7)?

26) Do you think Sir Toby likes Maria? Write down two quotes to back up your opinion.

27) Who does Maria describe as "the trout that must be caught with tickling"?

28) Write down four insulting things that Sir Toby says about Malvolio.

29) In Scene 5 there are several characters on stage. Who is Malvolio talking to?

30) What kind of future is Malvolio imagining for himself?

31) What name is signed at the bottom of the letter?

32) How does the letter tell Malvolio to behave with servants?

33) What type of clothes does the letter suggest Malvolio should wear?

34) Give a modern-day translation of "gull-catcher" (Scene 5, line 165).

ACT 3 SCENE 1
Olivia's garden

> Viola comes to see Olivia. Olivia's really fallen for Cesario and Viola has to try and put Olivia off without revealing her disguise.

Enter VIOLA *and* FESTE, *playing on a pipe and* tabor

> tabor = small drum

VIOLA Save thee, friend, and thy music! Dost thou live by thy tabor?

FESTE No, sir, I live by the church.

VIOLA Art thou a churchman?

> 4 Viola's being playful here — she knows Feste's not a priest because he's wearing a fool's outfit.

FESTE No such matter, sir. I do live by the church — for I do live 5 at my house, and my house doth stand by the church.

> lies by = sleeps with
>
> stands by = is supported by

VIOLA So thou mayst say the king lies by a beggar, if a beggar dwell near him — or the church stands by thy tabor if thy tabor stand by the church.

FESTE You have said, sir. To see this age! A sentence is but a 10 cheveril glove to a good wit — how quickly the wrong side may be turned outward!

> 10-12 'A clever person can turn a sentence inside out like a kid glove.'

VIOLA Nay, that's certain: they that dally nicely with words may quickly make them wanton.

> 13-14 'People who mess around with words make them loose.'

FESTE I would therefore my sister had had no name, sir. 15

VIOLA Why, man?

FESTE Why, sir, her name's a word, and to dally with that word might make my sister wanton — but, indeed, words are very rascals, since bonds disgraced them.

> 17-19 'I wish my sister didn't have a name — because messing around with that word might make her immoral.'

VIOLA Thy reason, man? 20

FESTE Truth, sir, I can yield you none without words, and words are grown so false, I am loath to prove reason with them.

> 21-22 'You can't tell the truth without words, but words are so flexible that I don't think I can be logical with them.'

VIOLA I warrant thou art a merry fellow and car'st for nothing.

FESTE Not so, sir, I do care for something — but in my conscience, sir, I do not care for you: if that be to care for 25 nothing, I would it would make you invisible.

VIOLA Art not thou the Lady Olivia's fool?

FESTE No, indeed, sir. The Lady Olivia has no folly. She will keep no fool, sir, till she be married, and fools are as like husbands as pilchards are to herrings — the husband's the 30 bigger. I am indeed not her fool but her corrupter of words.

> 28-31 'Olivia won't have a fool till she gets married. Fools and husbands are like pilchards and herrings — husbands are bigger.'

VIOLA I saw thee late at the Count Orsino's.

> late = lately
>
> orb = planet

FESTE Foolery, sir, does walk about the orb like the sun — it shines everywhere. I would be sorry, sir, but the fool should be as oft with your master as with my mistress — I think I saw your 35 wisdom there.

VIOLA Nay, and thou pass upon me, I'll no more with thee. Hold, there's expenses for thee.

> 37-38 'You're making a fool of me — I won't stay here. Wait, here's some money for you.'

Gives a coin

FESTE Now Jove, in his next commodity of hair, send thee a beard! 40

> commodity = hand-out

VIOLA By my troth, I'll tell thee, I am almost sick for one — *(Aside)* though I would not have it grow on my chin. Is thy lady within?

FESTE Would not a pair of these have bred, sir?

> 44 'If only a couple of these coins would have children.' i.e. 'Give me more money.'

30

use = lending money for interest

46-47 'I'd be a go-between if you gave me one more coin.' Feste could mean he's going to matchmake the two coins, or Cesario and Olivia. In the story of Troilus and Cressida, Lord Pandarus is their go-between.

50-52 'I'll explain to them that you're from Orsino. Who you are and what you want is none of my business.'

54-57 'This bloke's clever enough to be a fool; playing the fool does take brains of a sort. You have to think about the audience's mood, what sort of people they are, and the occasion.'

haggard = untrained hawk

check at = snap at

59-62 'It's as hard as the jobs that wise men do. When he's foolish it's on purpose. When wise men are foolish you wonder how clever they really are.'

65 'God keep you, sir.'
66 'And you too — your servant.'

encounter = enter

list = destination

understand = stand under

Yuk!

76-77 'I will take steps and enter — but we can't go in (here comes Olivia).'

odours = sweet fragrances

rare = outstanding

81-82 'My message is only for your ready and willing ear.'

83-84 'I'll make a note of those words.'

Mellifluous
Pregnant
Vouchsafe
Odors odours

Andrew's book of nifty words

VIOLA Yes, being kept together and put to use. 45

FESTE I would play Lord Pandarus of Phrygia, sir, to bring a Cressida to this Troilus.

VIOLA I understand you sir — 'tis well begged.

Gives another coin

FESTE The matter, I hope, is not great, sir — begging but a beggar: Cressida was a beggar. My lady is within, sir. I will 50 construe to them whence you come; who you are, and what you would, are out of my welkin — I might say 'element', but the word is overworn.

Exit

VIOLA This fellow is wise enough to play the fool,
And to do that well craves a kind of wit; 55
He must observe their mood on whom he jests,
The quality of persons, and the time —
Not, like the haggard, check at every feather
That comes before his eye. This is a practice,
As full of labour as a wise man's art: 60
For folly that he wisely shows is fit —
But wise men, folly-fallen, quite taint their wit.

Enter SIR TOBY *and* SIR ANDREW

SIR TOBY Save you, gentleman.

VIOLA And you, sir.

SIR ANDREW *Dieu vous garde, monsieur.* 65

VIOLA *Et vous aussi; votre serviteur.*

SIR ANDREW I hope, sir, you are, and I am yours.

SIR TOBY Will you encounter the house? My niece is desirous you should enter, if your trade be to her.

VIOLA I am bound to your niece, sir — I mean, she is the list of 70 my voyage.

SIR TOBY Taste your legs, sir — put them to motion.

VIOLA My legs do better understand me, sir, than I understand what you mean by bidding me taste my legs.

SIR TOBY I mean, to go, sir, to enter. 75

VIOLA I will answer you with gait and entrance — but we are prevented.

Enter OLIVIA *and* MARIA

Most excellent accomplished lady, the heavens rain odours on you!

SIR ANDREW That youth's a rare courtier — 'rain odours' — well. 80

VIOLA My matter hath no voice, lady, but to your own most pregnant and vouchsafed ear.

SIR ANDREW 'Odours', 'pregnant', and 'vouchsafed': I'll get 'em all three all ready.

OLIVIA Let the garden door be shut, and leave me to my 85 hearing.

Exeunt SIR TOBY, SIR ANDREW, *and* MARIA

Give me your hand, sir.

VIOLA   My duty, madam, and most humble service.

OLIVIA   What is your name?

VIOLA   Cesario is your servant's name, fair princess.   90

OLIVIA   My servant, sir? 'Twas never merry world
    Since lowly feigning was called compliment.
    Y'are servant to the Count Orsino, youth.

lowly feigning = pretending to be respectful

VIOLA   And he is yours, and his must needs be yours —
    Your servant's servant is your servant, madam.   95

OLIVIA   For him, I think not on him — for his thoughts,
    Would they were blanks, rather than filled with me!

96-97 'I don't think about Orsino, and I'd rather he had no thoughts at all than thought about me!'

VIOLA   Madam, I come to whet your gentle thoughts
    On his behalf.

whet = sharpen, make keener

OLIVIA   O by your leave, I pray you!
    I bade you never speak again of him —   100
    But would you undertake another suit
    I had rather hear you to solicit that,
    Than music from the spheres.

101-103 'If you would flirt for someone else, I'd rather listen to you than to the music of heaven.'

VIOLA   Dear lady —

OLIVIA   Give me leave, beseech you. I did send,
    After the last enchantment you did here,   105
    A ring in chase of you. So did I abuse
    Myself, my servant, and, I fear me, you.

104-106 'After the last spell you cast on me I sent you a ring.'

    Under your hard construction must I sit,
    To force that on you in a shameful cunning
    Which you knew none of yours. What might you think?   110

108-110 'You must think badly of me for forcing you to accept the ring (which you knew wasn't yours) in such a devious way.'

    Have you not set mine honour at the stake,
    And baited it with all th' unmuzzled thoughts
    That tyrannous heart can think? To one of your receiving
    Enough is shown — a cypress, not a bosom,
    Hides my heart — so, let me hear you speak.   115

111-115 'Haven't you ripped my honour to shreds in your thoughts, like a dog at a bear-baiting? I've said enough, I'm going to hide my feelings. It's your turn to speak.'

VIOLA   I pity you.

OLIVIA   That's a degree to love.

VIOLA   No, not a grise — for 'tis a vulgar proof
    That very oft we pity enemies.

117-118 'Not at all — it's common knowledge that people often pity their enemies.'

OLIVIA   Why then, methinks 'tis time to smile again.
    O world, how apt the poor are to be proud!   120
    If one should be a prey, how much the better
    To fall before the lion than the wolf!

120 'Those who have nothing can still be proud!'

121-122 'Better to be the victim of a noble lion than of a hungry wolf.'

                Clock strikes

    The clock upbraids me with the waste of time.
    Be not afraid, good youth; I will not have you —
    And yet when wit and youth is come to harvest,   125
    Your wife is like to reap a proper man.
    There lies your way, due west.

upbraids me with = tells me off for

125-126 'When you have grown to maturity, your wife will harvest a decent man.'

VIOLA   Then westward ho!
    Grace and good disposition attend your ladyship!
    You'll nothing, madam, to my lord by me?

OLIVIA   Stay!   130
    I prithee tell me what thou think'st of me.

VIOLA   That you do think you are not what you are.

132 'You think you are something you are not.'

Act 3, Scene 1

OLIVIA If I think so, I think the same of you.

VIOLA Then think you right: I am not what I am.

OLIVIA I would you were as I would have you be.   135

VIOLA Would it be better, madam, than I am?
I wish it might, for now I am your fool.

OLIVIA *(Aside)* O what a deal of scorn looks beautiful
In the contempt and anger of his lip!

140-141 *'It's even harder to hide love than it is to hide a guilty conscience. Even when lovers are being secretive it's obvious what they're up to.'*

A murderous guilt shows not itself more soon,   140
Than love that would seem hid. Lovers' night is noon.
Cesario, by the roses of the spring,
By maidhood, honour, truth, and everything,

maugre = despite

I love thee so that, maugre all thy pride,
Nor wit nor reason can my passion hide.   145

146-149 *'Don't think that because I'm wooing you, you shouldn't be interested in me. It's good to be given love when you've asked for it, but it's better to be loved when you didn't expect it.'*

Do not extort thy reasons from this clause,
For that I woo, thou therefore hast no cause —
But rather reason thus with reason fetter:
Love sought is good, but given unsought is better.

Eek - I'd really better be going now.

fetter = chain up

VIOLA By innocence I swear, and by my youth,   150
I have one heart, one bosom, and one truth,

151-153 *'I have one heart, and it doesn't belong to any woman — its only mistress is me.'*

And that no woman has — nor never none
Shall mistress be of it, save I alone.
And so, adieu, good madam — never more
Will I my master's tears to you deplore.   155

deplore = declare

OLIVIA Yet come again: for thou perhaps mayst move
That heart which now abhors to like his love.

Exeunt

ACT 3 SCENE 2
Olivia's house

Enter SIR TOBY, SIR ANDREW, *and* FABIAN.

Sir Andrew's seen Olivia and Cesario together, and he gets jealous. Sir Toby tells Sir Andrew to challenge Cesario to a duel, and Sir Toby tells Fabian he's been living off Sir Andrew's money. Malvolio becomes even more annoying now that he's started wearing yellow stockings.

SIR ANDREW No, faith, I'll not stay a jot longer.

jot = bit

SIR TOBY Thy reason, dear venom, give thy reason.

venom = fury

FABIAN You must needs yield your reason, Sir Andrew.

4-5 *'Your niece was being nicer to Cesario than she's ever been to me.'*

SIR ANDREW Marry, I saw your niece do more favours to the count's serving-man than ever she bestowed upon me; I saw't i' the orchard.   5

7 *'Did she see you?'*

SIR TOBY Did she see thee the while, old boy? Tell me that.

SIR ANDREW As plain as I see you now.

argument = proof

FABIAN This was a great argument of love in her toward you.   10

'Slight! = by God's light!

SIR ANDREW 'Slight! Will you make an ass o' me?

legitimate = true

FABIAN I will prove it legitimate, sir, upon the oaths of judgment and reason.

grand-jurymen = true witnesses

SIR TOBY And they have been grand-jurymen since before Noah was a sailor.   15

16-18 *'She was only friendly to Cesario to get you all worked up.'*

FABIAN She did show favour to the youth in your sight only to exasperate you, to awake your dormouse valour, to put fire in your heart and brimstone in your liver. You should then

dormouse = small, weedy

have accosted her — and with some excellent jests, fire-new
from the mint, you should have banged the youth into   20
dumbness. This was looked for at your hand, and this was
balked: the double gilt of this opportunity you let time wash
off, and you are now sailed into the north of my lady's
opinion — where you will hang like an icicle on a
Dutchman's beard, unless you do redeem it by some   25
laudable attempt either of valour or policy.

SIR ANDREW And't be any way, it must be with valour — for
policy I hate: I had as lief be a Brownist as a politician.

SIR TOBY Why, then, build me thy fortunes upon the basis
of valour. Challenge me the count's youth to fight with   30
him — hurt him in eleven places: my niece shall take note of
it — and assure thyself, there is no love-broker in the world
can more prevail in man's commendation with woman than
report of valour.

FABIAN
There is no way but this, Sir Andrew.   35

SIR ANDREW Will either of you bear me a challenge to him?

SIR TOBY Go, write it in a martial hand, be curst and brief — it
is no matter how witty, so it be eloquent and full of invention.
Taunt him with the licence of ink — if thou thou'st him
some thrice, it shall not be amiss — and as many lies as   40
will lie in thy sheet of paper, although the sheet were big
enough for the bed of Ware in England, set 'em down — go,
about it. Let there be gall enough in thy ink, though thou
write with a goose-pen, no matter — about it.

SIR ANDREW Where shall I find you?   45

SIR TOBY We'll call thee at the cubiculo — go.

Exit SIR ANDREW

FABIAN This is a dear manikin to you, Sir Toby.

SIR TOBY I have been dear to him, lad, some two thousand
strong, or so.

FABIAN We shall have a rare letter from him — but you'll not   50
deliver't?

SIR TOBY Never trust me, then; and by all means stir on the
youth to an answer. I think oxen and wainropes cannot
hale them together. For Andrew, if he were opened, and
you find so much blood in his liver as will clog the foot of a 55
flea, I'll eat the rest of the anatomy.

FABIAN And his opposite, the youth, bears in his visage no great
presage of cruelty.

Enter MARIA

SIR TOBY Look, where the youngest wren of nine comes.

MARIA If you desire the spleen, and will laugh yourself into   60
stitches, follow me. Yond gull Malvolio is turned heathen, a
very renegado — for there is no Christian, that means to be
saved by believing rightly, can ever believe such impossible
passages of grossness. He's in yellow stockings.

19-21 'You should have shown Cesario who's boss with some really great, brand-new wisecracks.'

21-26 'That's what you should have done, but you let it slip. You've wasted this brilliant opportunity and now Olivia will be cold towards you, unless you pull off some kind of impressive stunt.'

policy = strategy

as lief = as gladly

Brownist: Sir Andrew is prejudiced against a funny sect founded by Robert Browne in 1581.

30-31 'Challenge Cesario to a duel.'

32-34 'Women love nothing more than a brave man.'

bear = deliver

martial hand = aggressive, military style

curst = fierce

invention = imagination, or lies

39-42 'Write as much to annoy Cesario as you can. Fill the paper, even if it's as big as the biggest bed in England.'

gall = cheekiness

goose-pen = quill

cubiculo = bedroom

dear manikin = friendly puppet

48-49 'Dear' means 'expensive' here — Sir Toby's saying that he's spent a lot of Sir Andrew's money.

52-53 'pressure Cesario to answer Sir Andrew's challenge.'

wainropes = wagon-ropes

hale = drag

54-56 'If you cut Andrew up, I bet you wouldn't find any blood in him.' (a sign of cowardice)

57-58 'And Cesario doesn't show a hint of cruelty.'

the youngest wren of nine = a tiny tiny bird

spleen = fit of laughter

yond gull = that fool

heathen, renegado = unbeliever in religion

impossible passages of grossness = massive impossibilities

Act 3, Scene 2

SIR TOBY And cross-gartered?   65

MARIA Most villainously. Like a pedant that keeps a school i' th'
church. I have dogged him, like his murderer. He does obey
every point of the letter that I dropped to betray him. He
does smile his face into more lines than is in the new map
with the augmentation of the Indies — you have not seen   70
such a thing as 'tis. I can hardly forbear hurling things at him.
I know my lady will strike him. If she do, he'll smile and
take't for a great favour.

SIR TOBY Come, bring us, bring us where he is.

Exeunt

ACT 3 SCENE 3
A Street

Enter SEBASTIAN *and* ANTONIO

SEBASTIAN I would not by my will have troubled you. But,
since you make your pleasure of your pains, I will no further
chide you.

ANTONIO I could not stay behind you. My desire,
More sharp than filed steel, did spur me forth —   5
And not all love to see you, though so much
As might have drawn one to a longer voyage,
But jealousy what might befall your travel,
Being skilless in these parts — which to a stranger,
Unguided and unfriended, often prove   10
Rough and unhospitable: my willing love,
The rather by these arguments of fear,
Set forth in your pursuit.

SEBASTIAN   My kind Antonio,
I can no other answer make but thanks,
And thanks — and ever thanks; and oft good turns   15
Are shuffled off with such uncurrent pay —
But, were my worth as is my conscience firm,
You should find better dealing. What's to do?
Shall we go see the relics of this town?

ANTONIO Tomorrow, sir — best first go see your lodging.   20

SEBASTIAN I am not weary, and 'tis long to night.
I pray you, let us satisfy our eyes
With the memorials and the things of fame
That do renown this city.

ANTONIO Would you'd pardon me —   25
I do not without danger walk these streets.
Once, in a sea-fight, 'gainst the Count his galleys
I did some service — of such note indeed,
That were I ta'en here it would scarce be answered.

SEBASTIAN Belike you slew great number of his people.   30

ANTONIO The offence is not of such a bloody nature;
Albeit the quality of the time and quarrel
Might well have given us bloody argument.
I might have since been answered in repaying

---

pedant = *schoolmaster*

68-71 *'He believes every word of the letter I wrote. He keeps smiling like an idiot.'*

forbear = *hold back from*

Antonio catches up with Sebastian to see if he's OK. Sebastian wants to go sightseeing, but Antonio's scared he'll be seen and captured because he once fought in a battle against Orsino's men, and didn't pay compensation. Antonio gives Sebastian his purse to buy something nice, and they arrange to meet at the inn.

1-3 *'I didn't want to bother you. But, since you're happy to put yourself out, I'll stop banging on about it.'*

Hooray! I found you again!

Calm down. It's only been 19 pages since you last saw me.

jealousy = *fear*

skilless in = *unfamiliar with*

9-11 *'This country can be dangerous for people who don't know it.'*

11-13 *'I set out to follow you because I was afraid what might happen.'*

15-18 *'Often good turns are poorly rewarded with worthless pay — but if I were richer, I'd reward you properly.'*

relics = *famous buildings*

21-24 *'I'm not tired, and it's not bedtime for ages. Come on, let's go and see the sights.'*

25-29 *'I'll have to take a raincheck. I'm in danger here because I was once in a fight against Orsino's men. If I'm captured I won't escape punishment.'*

ta'en = *taken*

belike = *perhaps*

slew = *killed*

31-33 *'It wasn't as bloody as it might have been.'*

What we took from them — which, for traffic's sake,   35
Most of our city did. Only myself stood out,
For which, if I be lapsed in this place,
I shall pay dear.

SEBASTIAN   Do not then walk too open.

ANTONIO   It doth not fit me. Hold, sir, here's my purse.
In the south suburbs, at the Elephant,   40
Is best to lodge: I will bespeak our diet,
Whiles you beguile the time and feed your knowledge
With viewing of the town: there shall you have me.

SEBASTIAN   Why I your purse?

ANTONIO   Haply your eye shall light upon some toy   45
You have desire to purchase — and your store,
I think, is not for idle markets, sir.

SEBASTIAN   I'll be your purse-bearer and leave you for
An hour.

ANTONIO   To the Elephant.

SEBASTIAN   I do remember.

Exeunt

ACT 3 SCENE 4
Olivia's garden

Enter OLIVIA *followed by* MARIA

OLIVIA   (*Aside*) I have sent after him; he says he'll come —
How shall I feast him? What bestow of him?
For youth is bought more oft than begged or borrowed.
I speak too loud —
Where's Malvolio? He is sad and civil,   5
And suits well for a servant with my fortunes.
Where is Malvolio?

MARIA   He's coming, madam, but in very strange manner. He
is sure possessed, madam.

OLIVIA   Why, what's the matter? Does he rave?   10

MARIA   No, madam, he does nothing but smile. Your ladyship
were best to have some guard about you, if he come, for
sure the man is tainted in's wits.

OLIVIA   Go call him hither.

Exit MARIA

I am as mad as he
If sad and merry madness equal be.   15

Enter MARIA with MALVOLIO

How now, Malvolio?

MALVOLIO   Sweet lady, ho, ho!

OLIVIA   Smil'st thou? I sent for thee upon a sad occasion.

MALVOLIO   Sad, lady? I could be sad. This does make some
obstruction in the blood, this cross-gartering, but what of   20
that? If it please the eye of one, it is with me as the very true
sonnet is: 'Please one, and please all.'

Side notes:

traffic = *trade*

stood out = *didn't pay*

lapsed = *captured*

39 'I'll be careful.'
the Elephant = *the name of an inn*

41-43 'I'll order us some grub while you pass the time sightseeing.'

44 'Why do I need your purse?'

45-47 'Maybe you'll spot something you want to buy — and you don't have enough money for buying nice things.'

Olivia calls for Malvolio who's behaving very odd. Olivia leaves Maria and Sir Toby to look after him. Sir Andrew and Viola/Cesario are about to fight when Antonio turns up and saves the day.

2-3 'How will I entertain him? What will I give him? Young people are more impressed by presents than begging and pleading.'

5-6 'He's serious and polite, and the right kind of servant for someone like me.'

possessed = *mad, possessed by the devil*

11-13 'Be on your guard — he's lost his wits.'

I can't feel my feet - this had better be worth it.

19-22 'This cross-gartering's cutting off my circulation, but so what? If you're happy I'm happy.'

black in my mind = *sad*

25-27 *'Someone found the you-know-what, and the orders will be obeyed. I know that lovely handwriting.'*

oft = *often*

33 *'Nightingales, which are noble birds, will answer ordinary jackdaws.'*

To darling Malvolio,
Olivia wrote this, honest.
Love from Maria
Olivia

36 Malvolio's quoting from the letter Maria wrote.

I think I'm going mad...wibble...

midsummer madness: *it was believed people were more likely to go mad in midsummer*

entreat him back = *persuade him to come back*

57 *'get someone to look after Malvolio.'*

miscarry = *come to any harm*

concurs directly = *agrees exactly*

reverend carriage = *dignified bearing*

OLIVIA   Why, how dost thou, man? What is the matter with thee?

MALVOLIO   Not black in my mind, though yellow in my legs. It 25 did come to his hands, and commands shall be executed. I think we do know the sweet Roman hand.

OLIVIA   Wilt thou go to bed, Malvolio?

MALVOLIO   To bed? Ay, sweetheart, and I'll come to thee.

OLIVIA   God comfort thee! Why dost thou smile so and kiss thy 30 hand so oft?

MARIA   How do you, Malvolio?

MALVOLIO   At your request! Yes, nightingales answer daws!

MARIA   Why appear you with this ridiculous boldness before my lady? 35

MALVOLIO   'Be not afraid of greatness': 'twas well writ.

OLIVIA   What meanest thou by that, Malvolio?

MALVOLIO   'Some are born great —'

OLIVIA   Ha?

MALVOLIO   'Some achieve greatness —' 40

OLIVIA   What say'st thou?

MALVOLIO   'And some have greatness thrust upon them'

OLIVIA   Heaven restore thee!

MALVOLIO   'Remember who commended thy yellow stockings —' 45

OLIVIA   Thy yellow stockings?

MALVOLIO   'And wished to see thee cross-gartered.'

OLIVIA   Cross-gartered?

MALVOLIO   'Go to, thou art made, if thou desir'st to be so —'

OLIVIA   Am I made? 50

MALVOLIO   'If not, let me see thee a servant still.'

OLIVIA   Why, this is very midsummer madness.

Enter SERVANT

SERVANT   Madam, the young gentleman of the Count Orsino's is returned — I could hardly entreat him back.
He attends your ladyship's pleasure. 55

OLIVIA   I'll come to him.

Exit SERVANT

Good Maria, let this fellow be looked to. Where's my cousin Toby? Let some of my people have a special care of him — I would not have him miscarry for the half of my dowry.

Exeunt OLIVIA *and* MARIA

MALVOLIO   O ho! Do you come near me now? No worse man 60 than Sir Toby to look to me! This concurs directly with the letter: she sends him on purpose that I may appear stubborn to him — for she incites me to that in the letter. 'Cast thy humble slough,' says she; 'be opposite with a kinsman, surly with servants, let thy tongue tang with arguments of state, 65 put thyself into the trick of singularity,' and consequently sets down the manner how: as a sad face, a reverend carriage, a

slow tongue, in the habit of some sir of note, and so forth. I
have limed her, but it is Jove's doing, and Jove make me
thankful! And when she went away now, 'Let this fellow be   70
looked to' – 'fellow'! Not Malvolio, nor after my degree, but
'fellow.' Why, everything adheres together, that no dram of
a scruple, no scruple of a scruple, no obstacle, no
incredulous or unsafe circumstance – what can be said?
Nothing that can be can come between me and the full   75
prospect of my hopes. Well, Jove, not I, is the doer of this,
and he is to be thanked!

Enter SIR TOBY, FABIAN, *and* MARIA

SIR TOBY Which way is he, in the name of sanctity? If all the
devils of hell be drawn in little, and Legion himself possessed
him, yet I'll speak to him.   80

FABIAN Here he is, here he is. How is't with you, sir?

SIR TOBY How is't with you, man?

MALVOLIO Go off, I discard you. Let me enjoy my private.
Go off!

MARIA Lo, how hollow the fiend speaks within him! Did not I   85
tell you? Sir Toby, my lady prays you to have a care of him.

MALVOLIO Ah ha! Does she so?

SIR TOBY Go to, go to; peace, peace! We must deal gently
with him. Let me alone. How do you, Malvolio? How is't
with you? What, man, defy the devil! Consider, he's an   90
enemy to mankind.

MALVOLIO Do you know what you say?

MARIA La you! And you speak ill of the devil, how he takes it
at heart! Pray God he be not bewitched!

FABIAN Carry his water to th' wise woman.   95

MARIA Marry, and it shall be done tomorrow morning if I live.
My lady would not lose him for more than I'll say.

MALVOLIO How now, mistress?

MARIA O Lord!

SIR TOBY Prithee, hold thy peace; this is not the way. Do you 100
not see you move him? Let me alone with him.

FABIAN No way but gentleness – gently, gently: the fiend is
rough, and will not be roughly used.

SIR TOBY Why, how now, my bawcock? How dost thou, chuck?

MALVOLIO Sir!   105

SIR TOBY Ay, biddy, come with me. What, man, 'tis not for
gravity to play at cherry-pit with Satan. Hang him, foul collier!

MARIA Get him to say his prayers, good Sir Toby, get him to
pray.

MALVOLIO My prayers, minx!   110

MARIA No, I warrant you, he will not hear of godliness.

MALVOLIO Go hang yourselves all! You are idle, shallow
things – I am not of your element. You shall know more
hereafter.

Exit

68-69 'I've caught her like a bird in a trap.'

fellow = companion

after my degree = in keeping with my status as a servant

72-74 'It all fits together — there can be no doubt.'

75-76 'There's nothing that can possibly come between me and what I hope for.'

78-80 'Even if he's possessed by all the devils in hell, I won't be stopped from speaking to him.'

83-84 'Get away! I won't be needing you. Leave me in peace!' Malvolio's talking to the others like they were his servants.

have a care of him = look after him

90 Toby's pretending he thinks Malvolio's possessed by a devil.

93-94 'Look! If you say bad things about the devil he gets upset! I pray to God he hasn't had a spell cast on him.'

95 'Take a urine sample to the wise woman — she'll know if he's been bewitched.'

Has anyone seen my urine sample?

100-101 'Please calm down, you're upsetting him. Leave me alone with him.'

bawcock = pretty bird

chuck, biddy = chicken

106-107 'Grown men shouldn't play kid's games with the devil.'

foul collier = filthy coalman

112-114 'Go hang yourselves! You are lazy, worthless sorts — I'm a cut above you lot. You'll see.'

Act 3, Scene 4

38

116-117 'If this was a play, I'd say it was completely unrealistic.'

118-119 'He's completely fallen for the trick.'

genius = soul

120 'Follow him, quick, in case he realises what's going on when he has a moment to himself.'

123 'We'll tie him up and put him in a darkened room.'

124-128 'We'll carry on enjoying ourselves, and punishing him, until the trick runs out of steam, and we feel sorry for him. Then we'll bring it all out into the open.'

129 'More loopiness!'

challenge = invitation to fight a duel

saucy = spicy

scurvy fellow = wretched individual

137-138 'Don't question why I call you that. I'll give you no reason.'

139 'That'll keep you out of trouble with the law.'

143 'Very good — not.'

You're on the windy side of the law.

o' th' windy side of the law = safe from prosecution

153 'If that doesn't get him angry then nothing will.'

154-155 'The right moment's coming up — he's talking to Olivia and he'll be off soon.'

bum-baily = bailiff (bailiffs sneak up on you from behind)

158-161 'often a well-delivered curse makes you look more manly than actual manly behaviour.'

SIR TOBY Is't possible? 115

FABIAN If this were played upon a stage now, I could condemn it as an improbable fiction.

SIR TOBY His very genius hath taken the infection of the device, man.

MARIA Nay, pursue him now, lest the device take air and taint. 120

FABIAN Why, we shall make him mad indeed.

MARIA The house will be the quieter.

SIR TOBY Come, we'll have him in a dark room and bound. My niece is already in the belief that he's mad. We may carry it thus for our pleasure, and his penance, till our very 125 pastime, tired out of breath, prompt us to have mercy on him — at which time we will bring the device to the bar and crown thee for a finder of madmen. But see, but see!

Enter SIR ANDREW

FABIAN More matter for a May morning!

SIR ANDREW Here's the challenge; read it. I warrant there's 130 vinegar and pepper in't.

FABIAN Is't so saucy?

SIR ANDREW Ay, is't. I warrant him — do but read.

SIR TOBY Give me. *(Reads)* 'Youth, whatsoever thou art, thou art but a scurvy fellow.' 135

FABIAN Good, and valiant.

SIR TOBY *(Reads)* 'Wonder not, nor admire not in thy mind, why I do call thee so, for I will show thee no reason for't.'

FABIAN A good note! That keeps you from the blow of the law.

SIR TOBY *(Reads)* 'Thou com'st to the Lady Olivia, and in my 140 sight she uses thee kindly. But thou liest in thy throat. That is not the matter I challenge thee for.'

FABIAN Very brief, and to exceeding good sense *(Aside)* —less.

SIR TOBY *(Reads)* 'I will waylay thee going home, where if it be thy chance to kill me —' 145

FABIAN Good.

SIR TOBY *(Reads)* 'Thou killest me like a rogue and a villain.'

FABIAN Still you keep o' th' windy side of the law. Good.

SIR TOBY *(Reads)* 'Fare thee well, and God have mercy upon one of our souls! He may have mercy upon mine, but my 150 hope is better, and so look to thyself. Thy friend, as thou usest him, and thy sworn enemy,

Andrew Aguecheek.'

If this letter move him not, his legs cannot. I'll give't him.

MARIA You may have very fit occasion for't; he is now in some commerce with my lady and will by and by depart. 155

SIR TOBY Go, Sir Andrew, scout me for him at the corner of the orchard like a bum-baily. So soon as ever thou seest him, draw, and as thou draw'st, swear horrible; for it comes to pass oft that a terrible oath, with a swaggering accent sharply twanged off, gives manhood more approbation than ever 160 proof itself would have earned him. Away!

Act 3, Scene 4

SIR ANDREW   Nay, let me alone for swearing.

Exit

SIR TOBY   Now will not I deliver his letter; for the behaviour of the young gentleman gives him out to be of good capacity and breeding — his employment between his lord and my niece confirms no less. Therefore this letter, being so excellently ignorant, will breed no terror in the youth; he will find it comes from a clodpole. But, sir, I will deliver his challenge by word of mouth, set upon Aguecheek a notable report of valour, and drive the gentleman (as I know his youth will aptly receive it) into a most hideous opinion of his rage, skill, fury, and impetuosity. This will so fright them both that they will kill one another by the look, like cockatrices.

165

170

FABIAN   Here he comes with your niece; give them way till he take leave and presently after him.

175

Enter OLIVIA *and* VIOLA

SIR TOBY   I will meditate the while upon some horrid message for a challenge.

Exeunt SIR TOBY, FABIAN *and* MARIA

OLIVIA   I have said too much unto a heart of stone,
And laid mine honour too unchary out —
There's something in me that reproves my fault,
But such a headstrong potent fault it is,
That it but mocks reproof.

180

VIOLA   With the same 'haviour that your passion bears
Goes on my master's griefs.

OLIVIA   Here, wear this jewel for me; 'tis my picture.
Refuse it not; it hath no tongue to vex you.
And, I beseech you, come again tomorrow.
What shall you ask of me that I'll deny,
That honour, saved, may upon asking give?

185

VIOLA   Nothing but this — your true love for my master.

190

OLIVIA   How with mine honour may I give him that
Which I have given to you?

VIOLA   I will acquit you.

OLIVIA   Well, come again tomorrow. Fare thee well.
A fiend like thee might bear my soul to hell.

Exit

Enter SIR TOBY *and* FABIAN

SIR TOBY   Gentleman, God save thee.

195

VIOLA   And you, sir.

SIR TOBY   That defence thou hast, betake thee to't. Of what nature the wrongs are thou hast done him, I know not — but thy intercepter, full of despite, bloody as the hunter, attends thee at the orchard-end. Dismount thy tuck, be yare in thy preparation, for thy assailant is quick, skilful, and deadly.

200

VIOLA   You mistake, sir. I am sure no man hath any quarrel to me. My remembrance is very free and clear from any image of offence done to any man.

Side notes:

166-168 'This letter's so badly written it won't scare the young man — he'll see it's from a blockhead.'

169-172 'I'll make out Andrew's a real he-man. The lad'll get a really scary picture of him.'

cockatrices = monstrous snakes that can kill with a stare

176-177 'I'll make up a really scary challenge.'

178-182 'I've thrown myself at someone who doesn't care. Part of me thinks I'm stupid, but my feelings are too strong.'

unchary = unsparingly

potent = powerful

183-184 'Orsino is as unhappy as you are.'

188-189 'Ask me for something. I'll give you anything, so long as I can give it, but keep my honour.'

191-192 'It wouldn't be honourable to give him something I've already given to you.'

197 'Defend yourself however you can.'

199-201 'Your attacker is waiting in the orchard, full of venom. Unsheath your sword, prepare yourself quickly...'

202-203 'I never did anything to anyone.'

40

SIR TOBY You'll find it otherwise, I assure you. Therefore, if 205
you hold your life at any price, betake you to your guard —
for your opposite hath in him what youth, strength, skill, and
wrath can furnish man withal.

VIOLA I pray you, sir, what is he?

SIR TOBY He is knight, dubbed with unhatched rapier, and on 210
carpet consideration, but he is a devil in private brawl. Souls
and bodies hath he divorced three, and his incensement at
this moment is so implacable that satisfaction can be none
but by pangs of death and sepulchre. Hob-nob is his word:
give't or take't. 215

VIOLA I will return again into the house and desire some
conduct of the lady. I am no fighter. I have heard of some
kind of men that put quarrels purposely on others to taste
their valour — belike this is a man of that quirk.

SIR TOBY Sir, no. His indignation derives itself out of a very 220
competent injury; therefore get you on and give him his
desire. Back you shall not to the house, unless you
undertake that with me which with as much safety you
might answer him; therefore on, or strip your sword stark
naked — for meddle you must, that's certain, or forswear to 225
wear iron about you.

VIOLA This is as uncivil as strange. I beseech you, do me this
courteous office as to know of the knight what my offence
to him is. It is something of my negligence, nothing of my
purpose. 230

SIR TOBY I will do so. Signior Fabian, stay you by this
gentleman till my return.

Exit SIR TOBY

VIOLA Pray you, sir, do you know of this matter?

FABIAN I know the knight is incensed against you, even to a
mortal arbitrement, but nothing of the circumstance more. 235

VIOLA I beseech you, what manner of man is he?

FABIAN Nothing of that wonderful promise, to read him by his
form, as you are like to find him in the proof of his valour.
He is indeed, sir, the most skilful, bloody, and fatal opposite
that you could possibly have found in any part of Illyria. 240
Will you walk towards him? I will make your peace with
him if I can.

VIOLA I shall be much bound to you for't. I am one that had
rather go with Sir Priest than Sir Knight. I care not who
knows so much of my mettle. 245

Exeunt

Enter SIR TOBY *and* SIR ANDREW

SIR TOBY Why, man, he's a very devil; I have not seen such a
firago. I had a pass with him, rapier, scabbard, and all, and
he gives me the stuck-in with such a mortal motion that it is
inevitable — and on the answer, he pays you as surely as your
feet hits the ground they step on. They say he has been 250
fencer to the Sophy.

Glosses (left margin):

205-206 'if you value your life at all'

207-208 'your opponent's got everything that youth, strength, skill and anger can give a man.'

210-211 'He was made knight with an unused sword, for work indoors, not on the battlefield'

211-214 'He's killed three people, and he's so angry now, that only death and the tomb will satisfy him.'

hob-nob = have or don't have (your life)

217-219 'I've heard of men who start fights with others to test their bravery — I suppose he's one of those.'

derives itself out of = is the result of

competent = real

225-226 'you've got to get involved, or give up wearing a sword altogether.' (Only gentlemen wore swords. Toby's saying Viola's not behaving like a gentleman.)

227-230 'At least, for politeness' sake, tell me what I've done to make this knight angry — it can't have been on purpose.'

234-235 'I know the knight's angry enough to fight to the death, but nothing more.'

manner = kind of

237-238 'To look at him you'd never think he was a brave man.'

opposite = enemy

241-242 'I'll go and try to calm him down for you.'

243-245 'I'd always rather negotiate than fight. I don't care who knows it.'

mettle = courage

firago = female warrior

rapier = sword

247-250 'I had a fencing bout with him — you can't avoid his thrusts.'

fencer to the Sophy = fencing instructor to the ruler of Persia

Act 3, Scene 4

SIR ANDREW Pox on't. I'll not meddle with him.

SIR TOBY Ay, but he will not now be pacified. Fabian can scarce hold him yonder.

SIR ANDREW Plague on't, and I thought he had been valiant, and so cunning in fence, I'd have seen him damned ere I'd have challenged him. Let him let the matter slip, and I'll give him my horse, grey Capilet. 255

SIR TOBY I'll make the motion. Stand here, make a good show on't. This shall end without the perdition of souls. 260
(Aside) Marry, I'll ride your horse as well as I ride you.

Enter FABIAN *and* VIOLA

(To Fabian) I have his horse to take up the quarrel. I have persuaded him the youth's a devil.

FABIAN He is as horribly conceited of him and pants and looks pale, as if a bear were at his heels. 265

SIR TOBY (To Viola) There's no remedy, sir. He will fight with you for's oath sake. Marry, he hath better bethought him of his quarrel, and he finds that now scarce to be worth talking of. Therefore, draw for the supportance of his vow. He protests he will not hurt you. 270

VIOLA (Aside) Pray God defend me! A little thing would make me tell them how much I lack of a man.

FABIAN Give ground if you see him furious.

SIR TOBY Come, Sir Andrew, there's no remedy: the gentleman will for his honour's sake have one bout with you; he cannot 275
by the duello avoid it, but he has promised me, as he is a gentleman and a soldier, he will not hurt you. Come on, to't.

SIR ANDREW Pray God he keep his oath!

VIOLA I do assure you, 'tis against my will.

They draw

Enter ANTONIO

ANTONIO

Drawing

Put up your sword! If this young gentlemen 280
Have done offence, I take the fault on me —
If you offend him, I for him defy you.

SIR TOBY You, sir? Why, what are you?

ANTONIO One, sir, that for his love dares yet do more
Than you have heard him brag to you he will. 285

SIR TOBY Nay, if you be an undertaker, I am for you.

Draws

Enter OFFICERS

FABIAN O good Sir Toby, hold! Here come the officers.

SIR TOBY (To Antonio) I'll be with you anon.

VIOLA (To Sir Andrew) Pray, sir, put your sword up, if you please. 290

SIR ANDREW Marry, will I, sir; and for that I promised you, I'll be as good as my word. He will bear you easily and reins well.

pox on't = *curse it*

pacified = *calmed down*

255-257 *'Damn, if I'd thought he was brave and a good fencer, I'd never have challenged him.'*

motion = *suggestion*

perdition = *loss*

horribly conceited = *terrified*

266-270 *'He'll fight you for the sake of his honour, but he's not that bothered about the quarrel any more and won't hurt you.'*

271-272 *'Crikey! I'm almost on the point of telling them that I'm a woman.'*

duello = *duelling rules*

282 *'I'll do his fighting for him.'*

286 *'If you're going to stick your nose in, I'll fight you.'*

undertaker = *someone who interferes in other people's business*

hold = *stop*

anon = *later*

292-293 *Sir Andrew's talking about his horse.*

Act 3, Scene 4

office = duty

suit = order

C

297-298 'I recognise you, even without your captain's uniform.'

necessity = tricky situation

300-306 Antonio asks Viola for his purse because he thinks Viola is Sebastian.

313-315 'I haven't got much, but I'll split what I've got on me with you. Look, here's half what's in my purse.'

317-321 'How is it I can't persuade you to help when you owe me so much? Don't make me miserable — I might end up reminding you of everything I've done for you.'

323-326 'I hate ingratitude more than any of the vices which infect us.'

330-332 'I saved him from death with feelings of holy love, and worshipped his image — I thought he would be worthy of it.'

335-336 'You've betrayed your good looks — you've got an ugly mind.'

1ST OFFICER   This is the man — do thy office.

2ND OFFICER   Antonio, I arrest thee at the suit   295
Of Count Orsino.

ANTONIO   You do mistake me, sir.

1ST OFFICER   No, sir, no jot. I know your favour well,
Though now you have no sea-cap on your head.
Take him away; he knows I know him well.

ANTONIO   I must obey. *(To Viola)* This comes with seeking you. 300
But there's no remedy — I shall answer it.
What will you do, now my necessity
Makes me to ask you for my purse? It grieves me
Much more for what I cannot do for you
Than what befalls myself. You stand amazed,   305
But be of comfort.

2ND OFFICER   Come, sir, away.

ANTONIO   I must entreat of you some of that money.

VIOLA   What money, sir?
For the fair kindness you have showed me here,   310
And part being prompted by your present trouble,
Out of my lean and low ability
I'll lend you something. My having is not much —
I'll make division of my present with you.
Hold, there's half my coffer.   315

Offers him money

ANTONIO   Will you deny me now?

Refuses it

Is't possible that my deserts to you
Can lack persuasion? Do not tempt my misery,
Lest that it make me so unsound a man
As to upbraid you with those kindnesses   320
That I have done for you.

VIOLA   I know of none,
Nor know I you by voice or any feature.
I hate ingratitude more in a man
Than lying, vainness, babbling drunkenness,
Or any taint of vice whose strong corruption   325
Inhabits our frail blood.

ANTONIO   O heavens themselves!

2ND OFFICER   Come, sir, I pray you go.

ANTONIO   Let me speak a little. This youth that you see here,
I snatched one-half out of the jaws of death,
Relieved him with such sanctity of love;   330
And to his image, which methought did promise
Most venerable worth, did I devotion.

1ST OFFICER   What's that to us? The time goes by. Away!

ANTONIO   But O how vile an idol proves this god!
Thou hast, Sebastian, done good feature shame.   335
In nature there's no blemish but the mind:
None can be called deformed but the unkind.
Virtue is beauty, but the beauteous-evil

Are empty trunks, o'er-flourished by the devil.

1ST OFFICER   The man grows mad. Away with him! Come, 340
come, sir.

ANTONIO   Lead me on.

Exit (with OFFICERS)

VIOLA   Methinks his words do from such passion fly
That he believes himself — so do not I.
Prove true, imagination, O prove true, 345
That I, dear brother, be now ta'en for you!

SIR TOBY   Come hither, knight, come hither, Fabian. We'll
whisper o'er a couplet or two of most sage saws.

VIOLA   He named Sebastian. I my brother know
Yet living in my glass — even such and so 350
In favour was my brother, and he went
Still in this fashion, colour, ornament,
For him I imitate. O if it prove,
Tempests are kind, and salt waves fresh in love.

Exit

SIR TOBY   A very dishonest paltry boy, and more a coward 355
than a hare — his dishonesty appears in leaving his friend
here in necessity, and denying him; and for his cowardship,
ask Fabian.

FABIAN   A coward, a most devout coward, religious in it.

SIR ANDREW   'Slid, I'll after him again and beat him. 360

SIR TOBY   Do, cuff him soundly, but never draw thy sword.

SIR ANDREW   And I do not —

Exit

FABIAN   Come, let's see the event.

SIR TOBY   I dare lay any money, 'twill be nothing yet.

Exeunt

338-339 'beautiful people with evil characters are just hollow shells, made pretty by the devil.'

343-346 'If he's mistaken me for my brother, then maybe Sebastian's still alive!'

sage saws = *wise proverbs*

349-351 'I see my brother every time I look in the mirror — this is how he looked'

favour = *appearance*

paltry = *mean*

'Slid = *By God's eyelid!*

364 'I'll bet you any money that nothing will come of it.'

TONIGHT!
The Big Fight Live — Only on Cable

Act 3, Scene 4

43

Revision Summary — Act 3

You've made it this far, don't give up — the next two acts are really short. But first get your head round Act 3. Go through the act, answering these questions as you read through. Then try answering them again by memory and look up the ones you can't remember. It's a hard slog but the person who has to write an essay about this stuff is YOU.

1) Explain Feste's joke/pun that he "lives by the church" (Scene 1, lines 5-6).

2) Write out Feste's speech about husbands in your own words (Scene 1, lines 28-31).

3) Does Viola think that Feste is:
   a) a nuisance,   b) quite clever,   or c) religious?

4) Why is Viola visiting Olivia's house?

5) Describe Olivia's feelings for Viola in your own words.

6) Write out Viola's speech, Scene 1 lines 117-118, in your own words.

7) What is Viola hinting at when she says, "Then think you right: I am not what I am." (Scene 1, line 134)?

8) What does Olivia mean when she says, "Lovers' night is noon" (Scene 1, line 141)?

9) In Scene 2, why does Sir Andrew threaten to leave Olivia's house?

10) What reason does Fabian put forward for why Olivia was talking to Viola?

11) Which is the most likely reason why Sir Toby wants Sir Andrew to stay:
    a) he likes his wit,   b) he likes to borrow his money,   or c) he likes his cooking?

12) Whose idea is it for Sir Andrew to challenge Viola to a duel?

13) What does Sir Toby mean when he says about Sir Andrew and Viola, "I think oxen and wainropes cannot hale them together," (Scene 2, line 53-54)?

14) Write down three words Maria uses to describe Malvolio (Scene 2, lines 61-62).

15) What two reasons does Antonio give for following Sebastian?

16) Why is it dangerous for Antonio to be in Illyria?

17) What does Antonio give to Sebastian before they split up?

18) Which is most true of Sebastian and Antonio's relationship?
    a) Sebastian likes Antonio a lot, but Antonio is backing off.
    b) Antonio adores Sebastian, who is grateful but less keen.
    c) Sebastian is in love with Antonio, who couldn't care less.

19) Is Malvolio's entry in Scene 4 funny or sad for the audience? Why?

20) When Malvolio talks about greatness (Scene 4, lines 36-42), where is he quoting from?

21) What is Olivia's reaction to Malvolio's behaviour?

22) Why does Malvolio make an effort to be rude to Sir Toby in Scene 4, lines 83-84?

23) What does Sir Toby suggest should be done with Malvolio?

24) Is Sir Toby impressed by the challenge Sir Andrew has written to Viola? What does he do with the challenge?

25) What is the meaning of the word "unchary" (Scene 4, line 179)?

26) What's ironic about Viola trying to persuade Olivia to love Orsino?

27) Why does Antonio defend Viola when he has never met her before?

28) What does Antonio's mistake give Viola hope of (Scene 4, lines 349-354)?

ACT 4 SCENE 1
Outside Olivia's house

Enter SEBASTIAN *and* FESTE

> Feste thinks that Sebastian is Cesario, but Sebastian doesn't know Feste. Then Sir Andrew attacks Sebastian, and Sir Toby nearly starts a fight. Olivia butts in just in time, and invites Sebastian into her house.

FESTE Will you make me believe that I am not sent for you?

SEBASTIAN Go to, go to, thou art a foolish fellow,
Let me be clear of thee.

2-3 'Get lost, you twit.'

FESTE Well held out, i' faith! No, I do not know you, nor I am
not sent to you by my lady to bid you come speak with her;   5
nor your name is not Master Cesario — nor this is not my nose
neither. Nothing that is so, is so.

held out = kept up

7 'Nothing that seems real is real.'

SEBASTIAN I prithee, vent thy folly somewhere else,
Thou know'st not me.

8-9 'Please, tell your jokes somewhere else. You don't know me.'

FESTE Vent my folly! He has heard that word of some great   10
man and now applies it to a fool. Vent my folly! I am afraid
this great lubber, the world, will prove a cockney. I prithee
now, ungird thy strangeness and tell me what I shall vent to
my lady. Shall I vent to her that thou art coming?

lubber = awkward fool

cockney = spoilt kid

13 'stop pretending you don't know me'

14 'Shall I tell her you're coming?'

SEBASTIAN I prithee, foolish Greek, depart from me.   15
There's money for thee: if you tarry longer,
I shall give worse payment.

foolish Greek = silly joker

16-17 'Here's some money — if you hang around, I'll belt you one.'

FESTE By my troth, thou hast an open hand. These wise men
that give fools money get themselves a good report — after
fourteen years' purchase.   20

18 'Truly, you're ready to give money (or a punch) easily.'

19-20 'get themselves a good reputation — as long as they pay for it.'

Enter SIR ANDREW, SIR TOBY, *and* FABIAN

SIR ANDREW Now, sir, have I met you again? There's for you.

Strikes Sebastian

SEBASTIAN Why, there's for thee, and there, and there!

Beats Sir Andrew

Are all the people mad?

SIR TOBY Hold, sir, or I'll throw your dagger o'er the house.

24 'Stop fighting.'

FESTE This will I tell my lady straight: I would not be in some   25
of your coats for two pence.

25-26 'I'm glad I'm not in your shoes.'

Exit

SIR TOBY Come on, sir, hold!

SIR ANDREW Nay, let him alone, I'll go another way to work
with him; I'll have an action of battery against him, if there
be any law in Illyria. Though I struck him first, yet it's no   30
matter for that.

action of battery = assault charges

SEBASTIAN Let go thy hand!

SIR TOBY Come, sir, I will not let you go. Come, my young
soldier, put up your iron: you are well fleshed. Come on.

34 'draw your sword — you're experienced in fighting'

SEBASTIAN I will be free from thee. What wouldst thou now?   35
If thou dar'st tempt me further, draw thy sword.

35-36 'What do you want? Draw your sword if you think you're hard enough.'

SIR TOBY What, what! Nay, then I must have an ounce or two
of this malapert blood from you.

malapert = cheeky

Enter OLIVIA

OLIVIA Hold, Toby! On thy life I charge thee, hold!

hold = stop

SIR TOBY Madam!　　　　　　　　　　　　　　　　　40

OLIVIA Will it be ever thus? Ungracious wretch,
　　Fit for the mountains and the barbarous caves,
　　Where manners ne'er were preached! Out of my sight!
　　Be not offended, dear Cesario.
　　Rudesby, be gone!

Exeunt SIR TOBY, SIR ANDREW, *and* FABIAN

　　　　　　　　　I prithee, gentle friend,　　　45
　　Let thy fair wisdom, not thy passion, sway
　　In this uncivil and unjust extent
　　Against thy peace. Go with me to my house,
　　And hear thou there how many fruitless pranks
　　This ruffian hath botched up, that thou thereby　　50
　　May'st smile at this. Thou shalt not choose but go:
　　Do not deny. Beshrew his soul for me,
　　He started one poor heart of mine in thee.

SEBASTIAN What relish is in this? How runs the stream?
　　Or I am mad, or else this is a dream.　　　　　55
　　Let fancy still my sense in Lethe steep;
　　If it be thus to dream, still let me sleep!

OLIVIA Nay, come, I prithee; would thou'dst be ruled by me!

SEBASTIAN Madam, I will.

OLIVIA　　　　　　　　O, say so, and so be!

Exeunt

ACT 4 SCENE 2
Olivia's house

Enter MARIA *and* FESTE

MARIA Nay, I prithee, put on this gown and this beard; make
　　him believe thou art Sir Topas the curate. Do it quickly.
　　I'll call Sir Toby the whilst.

Exit

FESTE Well, I'll put it on, and I will dissemble myself in't, and I
　　would I were the first that ever dissembled in such a gown.　　5
　　I am not tall enough to become the function well, nor lean
　　enough to be thought a good student; but to be said an
　　honest man and a good housekeeper goes as fairly as to say
　　a careful man and a great scholar. The competitors enter.

Enter SIR TOBY *and* MARIA

SIR TOBY Jove bless thee, master Parson.　　　　　10

FESTE *Bonos dies*, Sir Toby. For, as the old hermit of Prague, that
　　never saw pen and ink, very wittily said to a niece of King
　　Gorboduc, 'That that is, is.' So I, being Master Parson, am
　　Master Parson; for what is 'that' but 'that'? And 'is' but 'is'?

SIR TOBY To him, Sir Topas.　　　　　　　　　15

FESTE What, ho, I say! Peace in this prison!

SIR TOBY The knave counterfeits well. A good knave.

MALVOLIO *(Within)* Who calls there?

Glossary / notes (margin):

ever thus = *always like this*

41-45 Olivia thinks that Sebastian is Cesario/Viola.

rudesby = *ruffian, bully*

46-48 'Don't get carried away in the heat of the moment of this rude and illegal attack.'

49-50 'how many cunning plans this bully's clumsily thought up.'

beshrew = *curse*

53 'He made my heart jump in fear.'

relish = *meaning*

56 'Let love make me forget everything.'

58 'will you do as I say?'

Maria gets Feste to dress up as a priest, and Feste tells Malvolio that he's mad even though he says he isn't. Then Sir Toby sends Feste in without the disguise. Malvolio still says he's not mad, and asks for pen and paper.

And tonight, Matthew, I'm going to be... a priest!

curate = *priest*

dissemble = *disguise*

function = *role of the priest*

7-9 'being called an honest and hospitable man is as good as being called a hardworking man and a good learner.'

bonos dies = *good day, in mock Latin*

King Gorboduc = *legendary king of Britain*

13-14 'Everything is as it seems. And I am a priest.'

counterfeits = *fakes it*

FESTE   Sir Topas the curate, who comes to visit Malvolio the
lunatic.   20

MALVOLIO   Sir Topas, Sir Topas, good Sir Topas, go to my lady.

FESTE   Out, hyperbolical fiend! How vexest thou this man!
Talkest thou nothing but of ladies?

22-23 'Get out, you crazy freak. You're really tormenting this man! Can't you talk about anything but women?'

SIR TOBY   Well said, Master Parson.

MALVOLIO   Sir Topas, never was man thus wronged. Good Sir   25
Topas, do not think I am mad. They have laid me here in
hideous darkness.

25 'There's never been a man treated as badly as me.'

FESTE   Fie, thou dishonest Satan! (I call thee by the most modest
terms, for I am one of those gentle ones that will use the
devil himself with courtesy.) Sayest thou that house is dark? 30

fie = expressing disgust

use = greet

house = room

MALVOLIO   As hell, Sir Topas.

FESTE   Why it hath bay windows, transparent as barricadoes,
and the clerestories toward the south-north are as lustrous as
ebony; and yet complainest thou of obstruction?

32-34 'But there are clear bay windows, and the upper windows are as bright as ebony — and you still complain about the darkness?'

MALVOLIO   I am not mad, Sir Topas. I say to you, this house is   35
dark.

FESTE   Madman, thou errest. I say, there is no darkness but
ignorance, in which thou art more puzzled than the
Egyptians in their fog.

thou errest = you are

38-39 'more lost than the Egyptians in the plague of darkness' — a story from the Bible.

MALVOLIO   I say, this house is as dark as ignorance, though   40
ignorance were as dark as hell; and I say there was never
man thus abused. I am no more mad than you are: make
the trial of it in any constant question.

42-43 'see if I'm mad by asking me some standard questions.'

FESTE   What is the opinion of Pythagoras concerning wildfowl?

MALVOLIO   That the soul of our grandam might haply inhabit   45
a bird.

45-46 'That my grandmother might be reincarnated as a bird.'

FESTE   What think'st thou of his opinion?

MALVOLIO   I think nobly of the soul, and no way approve his
opinion.

48-49 Malvolio is a devout Christian, and doesn't believe in reincarnation.

FESTE   Fare thee well. Remain thou still in darkness. Thou shalt   50
hold th' opinion of Pythagoras ere I will allow of thy wits,
and fear to kill a woodcock lest thou dispossess the soul of thy
grandam. Fare thee well.

50-53 'You'll have to believe Pythagoras before I certify you're not mad, and be scared to kill a woodcock in case it's your reincarnated grandmother.'

MALVOLIO   Sir Topas, Sir Topas!

SIR TOBY   My most exquisite Sir Topas!   55

exquisite = excellent

FESTE   Nay, I am for all waters.

56 'I can do anything.' Feste's being himself now.

MARIA   Thou mightst have done this without thy beard and
gown, he sees thee not.

57-58 'You needn't have bothered with the disguise — he can't even see you.'

SIR TOBY   To him in thine own voice, and bring me word how
thou findest him: I would we were well rid of this knavery.   60
If he may be conveniently delivered, I would he were, for I
am now so far in offence with my niece that I cannot
pursue with any safety this sport to the upshot. Come by
and by to my chamber.

59-60 'Go and speak to him without the disguise, and tell me how he's doing. I'll be glad to stop the trickery.'

61-64 'I'm in so much trouble with my niece that I can't continue with this trick. Come to my room later.'

upshot = end

Exeunt SIR TOBY *and* MARIA

FESTE   (*Singing*) Hey, Robin, jolly Robin,   65
Tell me how thy lady does.

On second thoughts, could you bring me my laptop computer?

74-75 'as always, you'll get money from me — just bring me stuff for writing.'

79 'how did you lose your senses?'

notoriously abused = badly treated

81 'I'm as sane as you are.'

propertied me = treated me like an object

asses = fools

86 'make me think I'm mad.'

advise you = be careful

89 'Try to go to sleep, and stop prattling.'

91 'Don't talk to him.'

Just wait til you see me do my Michael Caine impression.

shent = told off

well in my wits = sane

101 'I wish you were.'

convey = take

103-104 'You'll get more profit from it than you ever did for delivering a letter before.'

counterfeit = fake it

110 'I'll reward you well.'

anon = later

MALVOLIO Fool!

FESTE (*Singing*) My lady is unkind, perdy.

MALVOLIO Fool!

FESTE (*Singing*) Alas, why is she so? 70

MALVOLIO Fool, I say!

FESTE (*Singing*) She loves another —
Who calls, ha?

MALVOLIO Good fool, as ever thou wilt deserve well at my
hand, help me to a candle, and pen, ink and paper: as I am a 75
gentleman, I will live to be thankful to thee for't.

FESTE Master Malvolio?

MALVOLIO Ay, good fool.

FESTE Alas, sir, how fell you besides your five wits?

MALVOLIO Fool, there was never a man so notoriously abused. 80
I am as well in my wits, fool, as thou art.

FESTE But as well? Then you are mad indeed, if you be no better
in your wits than a fool.

MALVOLIO They have here propertied me: keep me in
darkness, send ministers to me, asses, and do all they can to 85
face me out of my wits.

FESTE Advise you what you say: the minister is here. (*As Sir
Topas*) Malvolio, Malvolio, thy wits the heavens restore.
Endeavour thyself to sleep, and leave thy vain bibble babble.

MALVOLIO Sir Topas! 90

FESTE (*As Sir Topas*) Maintain no words with him, good fellow.
(*As himself*) Who, I, sir? Not I, sir. God be wi' you, good Sir
Topas.
(*As Sir Topas*) Marry, amen.
(*As himself*) I will, sir, I will. 95

MALVOLIO Fool, fool, fool, I say!

FESTE Alas, sir, be patient. What say you sir? I am shent for
speaking to you.

MALVOLIO Good fool, help me to some light and some paper:
I tell thee, I am as well in my wits as any man in Illyria. 100

FESTE Well-a-day that you were, sir!

MALVOLIO By this hand, I am! Good fool, some ink, paper and
light, and convey what I will set down to my lady. It shall
advantage thee more than ever the bearing of letter did.

FESTE I will help you to't. But tell me true, are you not mad 105
indeed? Or do you but counterfeit?

MALVOLIO Believe me, I am not, I tell thee true.

FESTE Nay, I'll ne'er believe a madman till I see his brains. I will
fetch you light and paper and ink.

MALVOLIO Fool, I'll requite it in the highest degree. I prithee, be 110
gone.

FESTE (*Singing*)
I am gone, sir,
And anon, sir,
I'll be with you again,

In a trice,
Like to the old Vice,
   Your need to sustain;   115
Who, with dagger of lath,
In his rage and his wrath,
   Cries, 'Ah, ha!' to the devil: 120
Like a mad lad,
'Pare thy nails, dad,'
Adieu, good man devil!

Exit

trice = *moment*

old Vice = *character in medieval plays who cut the devil's nails with a dagger.*

lath = *wood*

wrath = *anger*

pare = *cut*

adieu = *goodbye*

How can I stoke the fires of Hell with fingernails like these?

ACT 4 SCENE 3
Olivia's garden
Enter SEBASTIAN

Sebastian's confused because he couldn't find Antonio, and now Olivia's coming on strong. Olivia turns up with a priest and asks Sebastian to marry her. Sebastian agrees straight away, and they go off to the chapel.

SEBASTIAN This is the air, that is the glorious sun,
This pearl she gave me, I do feel't and see't,
And though 'tis wonder that enwraps me thus,
Yet 'tis not madness. Where's Antonio, then?
I could not find him at the Elephant,   5
Yet there he was, and there I found this credit,
That he did range the town to seek me out.
His counsel now might do me golden service,
For though my soul disputes well with my sense,
That this may be some error, but no madness,   10
Yet doth this accident and flood of fortune
So far exceed all instance, all discourse,
That I am ready to distrust mine eyes,
And wrangle with my reason that persuades me
To any other trust but that I am mad,   15
Or else the lady's mad; yet, if 'twere so,
She could not sway her house, command her followers,
Take and give back affairs and their dispatch,
With such a smooth, discreet and stable bearing
As I perceive she does. There's something in't   20
That is deceivable. But here the lady comes.

Enter OLIVIA *and* PRIEST

OLIVIA Blame not this haste of mine. If you mean well,
Now go with me and with this holy man
Into the chantry by: there before him,
And underneath that consecrated roof,   25
Plight me the full assurance of your faith;
That my most jealous and too doubtful soul
May live at peace. He shall conceal it,
Whiles you are willing it shall come to note,
What time we will our celebration keep   30
According to my birth. What do you say?

SEBASTIAN I'll follow this good man, and go with you;
And, having sworn truth, ever will be true.

OLIVIA Then lead the way, good father, and heavens so shine,
That they may fairly note this act of mine!   35

Exeunt

2-4 *'I can feel and see this pearl that Olivia's given me, and even though everything seems crazy, I'm not mad.'*

was = *had been*

credit = *news*

range = *search*

8 *'His advice might help me out'*

disputes well = *agrees with*

11-16 *'Yet I've had so much more good luck than seems normal that I can hardly believe my eyes, and argue with my common sense that the only answer is that either I'm mad, or she is.'*

16-21 *'But if that were true, she wouldn't be able to rule her household and give orders to her servants with such easy behaviour as she seems to. There's something fishy going on here.'*

deceivable = *misleading*

22 *'Don't be put off by the speed of our marriage.'*

chantry by = *nearby chapel*

consecrated = *dedicated to religion*

plight = *pledge*

28-30 *'The priest will keep our marriage secret until you are happy for it to become known — then we'll have a proper party.'*

31 *'Do you agree?'*

33 *'When I've married you, I'll always be faithful.'*

34-35 *'May the heavens bless what I'm doing!'*

Revision Summary — Act 4

Act 4 is really nice and short, but there's <u>loads</u> going on. You've got to be absolutely sure about the plot (because it's getting VERY confusing by this point) — but that doesn't mean you can forget about the language and characters. You find out loads about Feste, Malvolio and Sebastian here — you've got to be able to prove your ideas about them with lines from the play. Keep going through these questions until you can answer them without needing to turn back to the play.

1) Where does Sebastian meet Feste in Scene 1?

2) Why is Feste confused when he meets Sebastian?

3) What does Sebastian think of Feste? Quote three phrases to back up your answer.

4) What does Feste mean when he says "nothing that is so, is so" (Scene 1, line 7)?

5) What does "vent thy folly" mean (Scene 1, line 8)?

6) What does Feste mean when he tells Sebastian to "ungird thy strangeness" (Scene 1, line 13)?

7) Explain the double meaning when Feste tells Sebastian that he has an "open hand" (Scene 1, line 18).

8) What do Sir Andrew and Sir Toby do to Sebastian when they meet him? What's Sebastian's reaction?

9) Who else arrives on stage with Sir Andrew and Sir Toby?

10) Who does Olivia call an "ungracious wretch" in line 41 of Scene 1?

11) Write out Olivia's speech in lines 45-53 of Scene 1 in your own words.

12) Where's the dark room where Malvolio gets locked up?

13) Who does Feste disguise himself as in Scene 2? Give his name and his job.

14) What does "dissemble" mean (Scene 2, line 4)?

15) What's the problem with Feste's phrase "bonos dies" (Scene 2, line 11)?

16) Would you describe Malvolio's mood in this scene as:
a) happy and excited, b) angry and upset or c) calm and thoughtful?

17) Explain the two arguments that the disguised Feste gives to show Malvolio that he's mad.

18) Who tells Feste to speak to Malvolio again, but without the disguise this time?

19) What does Sir Toby say about his relationship with Olivia in Scene 2?

20) What does Malvolio ask Feste to fetch for him?

21) Why does Feste mock Malvolio when Malvolio says "I am as well in my wits, fool, as thou art' (Scene 2, line 81)?

22) What does Malvolio mean when he says "they have here propertied me" (Scene 2, line 84)?

23) Feste asks Malvolio if he "counterfeits" (Scene 2, line 106). What does he mean?

24) What does "requite" mean (Scene 2, line 110)?

25) Why is Sebastian confused in Scene 3?

26) What's the news from the inn about Antonio?

27) Write out Sebastian's speech in lines 11-21 of Scene 3 in your own words.

28) Who arrives on stage with Olivia in Scene 3?

29) What does Olivia ask Sebastian to do in Scene 3?

30) What's a "chantry"? Is it:
a) a kind of song, b) a church c) an animal or d) an ancient Tibetan toilet?

ACT 5 SCENE 1
Olivia's garden

> In the final scene all the confusion gets cleared up, and they all live happily ever after — well, sort of.

Enter FESTE *and* FABIAN

FABIAN   Now, as thou lov'st me, let me see his letter.

    ← *1 'If you love me let me see Malvolio's letter.'*

FESTE   Good Master Fabian, grant me another request.

FABIAN   Anything.

FESTE   Do not desire to see this letter.

FABIAN   This is to give a dog, and in recompense desire my dog   5
    again.

    ← *5-6 'That's like giving me a dog, then asking for it back again.'*

Enter ORSINO, VIOLA, CURIO, *and Lords*

ORSINO   Belong you to the Lady Olivia, friends?

    ← *7 'Do you work for Lady Olivia?'*

FESTE   Ay, sir, we are some of her trappings.

    trappings = accessories

ORSINO   I know thee well. How dost thou, my good fellow?

FESTE   Truly, sir, the better for my foes, and the worse for my   10
    friends.

    foes = enemies

ORSINO   Just the contrary: the better for thy friends.

FESTE   No, sir, the worse.

ORSINO   How can that be?

FESTE   Marry, sir, they praise me, and make an ass of me. Now   15
    my foes tell me plainly I am an ass, so that by my foes, sir, I
    profit in the knowledge of myself, and by my friends I am
    abused. So that, conclusions to be as kisses, if your four
    negatives make your two affirmatives, why then, the worse
    for my friends and the better for my foes.   20

    ← *15 'My friends praise me too much — it makes me look stupid.'*

    ← *18-19 'Four negatives make two positives.'*

ORSINO   Why, this is excellent.

FESTE   By my troth, sir, no, though it please you to be one of my
    friends.

    ← *22-23 'On my honour, it's not — even if you are my friend.'*

ORSINO   Thou shalt not be the worse for me: there's gold.

FESTE   But that it would be double-dealing, sir, I would you   25
    could make it another.

    double-dealing = giving twice, or cheating

ORSINO   O you give me ill counsel.

    ← *27 'You give me bad advice'.*

FESTE   Put your grace in your pocket, sir, for this once, and let
    your flesh and blood obey it.

    ← *28-29 'Ignore your noble character, and let yourself obey my advice.'*

ORSINO   Well, I will be so much a sinner to be a double-dealer: 30
    there's another.

FESTE   *Primo, secundo, tertio*, is a good play, and the old saying
    is, 'The third pays for all' — the triplex, sir, is a good tripping
    measure; or the bells of Saint Bennet, sir, may put you in
    mind — one, two, three.   35

    Primo, secundo, tertio = Latin for 'First, second, third'.

    Triplex: a one-two-three dance rhythm.

ORSINO   You can fool no more money out of me at this throw.
    If you will let your lady know I am here to speak with her,
    and bring her along with you, it may awake my bounty further.

    at this throw = this time around

    ← *37-38 'Get Olivia to come out here and I might feel more generous.'*

FESTE   Marry, sir, lullaby to your bounty till I come again. I go,
    sir, but I would not have you to think that my desire of   40
    having is the sin of covetousness — but, as you say, sir, let your
    bounty take a nap. I will awake it anon.

    covetousness = greed

Exit

43 *Antonio rescued Viola from the duel with Sir Andrew.*

Vulcan = the gods' blacksmith in Roman myths

47-52 *'He was captain of a worthless little ship, but he caused our finest vessel such damage that envy itself praised him.'*

fraught from Candy = freight from Crete

57-58 *'We caught him brawling in the street, as though he couldn't care less about his reputation.'*

59-61 *'He drew his sword to help me, but then he spoke in a strange way — I don't know what it was, unless he was mad.'*

63-65 *'What on earth are you doing here, where you've made such bitter enemies?'*

on base and ground enough = with good reason

redeem = save

75-78 *'I came to this enemy town for Sebastian's sake, because I love him. I drew my sword to defend him when he was in trouble.'*

79-83 *'When I was arrested he didn't want to share my troubles, and all of a sudden pretended he'd never met me.'*

recommended to his use = lent him

interim = break

minute's vacancy = moment apart

VIOLA   Here comes the man, sir, that did rescue me.

Enter ANTONIO *and* OFFICERS

ORSINO   That face of his I do remember well;
Yet when I saw it last, it was besmeared   45
As black as Vulcan, in the smoke of war.
A baubling vessel was he captain of,
For shallow draught and bulk unprizable,
With which, such scathful grapple did he make
With the most noble bottom of our fleet,   50
That very envy, and the tongue of loss,
Cried fame and honour on him. What's the matter?

1ST OFFICER   Orsino, this is that Antonio
That took the Phoenix and her fraught from Candy,
And this is he that did the Tiger board,   55
When your young nephew Titus lost his leg.
Here in the streets, desperate of shame and state,
In private brabble did we apprehend him.

VIOLA   He did me kindness, sir, drew on my side,
But in conclusion put strange speech upon me,   60
I know not what 'twas, but distraction.

ORSINO   Notable pirate! Thou salt-water thief,
What foolish boldness brought thee to their mercies,
Whom thou, in terms so bloody and so dear,
Hast made thine enemies?

ANTONIO   Orsino, noble sir,   65
Be pleased that I shake off these names you give me.
Antonio never yet was thief or pirate,
Though I confess, on base and ground enough,
Orsino's enemy. A witchcraft drew me hither:
That most ungrateful boy there by your side,   70
From the rude sea's enraged and foamy mouth
Did I redeem. A wrack past hope he was.
His life I gave him, and did thereto add
My love without retention or restraint,
All his in dedication. For his sake,   75
Did I expose myself, pure for his love,
Into the danger of this adverse town,
Drew to defend him when he was beset;
Where being apprehended, his false cunning
(Not meaning to partake with me in danger)   80
Taught him to face me out of his acquaintance,
And grew a twenty years' removèd thing
While one would wink; denied me mine own purse,
Which I had recommended to his use
Not half an hour before.

VIOLA   How can this be?   85

ORSINO   When came he to this town?

ANTONIO   Today, my lord, and for three months before,
No interim, not a minute's vacancy,
Both day and night did we keep company.

Enter OLIVIA *and Attendants*

Act 5, Scene 1

ORSINO   Here comes the countess; now heaven walks on earth.   90
    But for thee, fellow — Fellow, thy words are madness.
    Three months this youth hath tended upon me,
    But more of that anon. Take him aside.

92 'This boy's been looking after me for three months.'

anon = later

OLIVIA   What would my lord, but that he may not have,
    Wherein Olivia may seem serviceable?   95
    Cesario, you do not keep promise with me.

94-96 'Is there any favour I can do you (apart from the one I can't)? Cesario, you've broken your vow.'

serviceable = of help

VIOLA   Madam!

ORSINO   Gracious Olivia —

OLIVIA   What do you say, Cesario? Good my lord —

VIOLA   My lord would speak, my duty hushes me.   100

OLIVIA   If it be aught to the old tune, my lord,
    It is as fat and fulsome to mine ear
    As howling after music.

101-103 'If you say anything you've said before I'll find it as ugly as howling after music.'

ORSINO   Still so cruel?

OLIVIA   Still so constant, lord.

constant = consistent

ORSINO   What, to perverseness? You uncivil lady,   105
    To whose ingrate and unauspicious altars
    My soul the faithfull'st off'rings have breathed out
    That e'er devotion tendered! What shall I do?

105-108 'Loyal to pig-headedness? Rude woman — I've offered you so much, but you're still ungrateful! What more can I do?'

OLIVIA   Even what it please my lord that shall become him.

109 'Do whatever you think suits you.'

ORSINO   Why should I not — had I the heart to do it —   110
    Like to th' Egyptian thief at point of death
    Kill what I love — a savage jealousy
    That sometimes savours nobly? But hear me this.
    Since you to non-regardance cast my faith,
    And that I partly know the instrument   115
    That screws me from my true place in your favour,
    Live you the marble-breasted tyrant still.
    But this your minion, whom I know you love,
    And whom, by heaven I swear, I tender dearly,
    Him will I tear out of that cruel eye   120
    Where he sits crownèd in his master's spite.
    Come, boy, with me; my thoughts are ripe in mischief.
    I'll sacrifice the lamb that I do love,
    To spite a raven's heart within a dove.

savours nobly = feels right

114-117 'Seeing as you don't care that I love you (and I know who's to blame), just carry on being cruel and cold-hearted.'

screws me = forces me away

marble-breasted = stone-hearted

118-121 'As for your little darling, I'll take him away from you. He enjoys your love in spite of me, his master.'

122-124 'Come Cesario, I'm full of ideas about how to punish you to get at Olivia.'

Leaving

VIOLA   And I most jocund, apt, and willingly,   125
    To do you rest, a thousand deaths would die.

125-126 'I'd happily die a thousand times over, to put your mind at rest.'

Following

OLIVIA   Where goes Cesario?

VIOLA   After him I love
    More than I love these eyes, more than my life,
    More, by all mores, than e'er I shall love wife.
    If I do feign, you witnesses above   130
    Punish my life for tainting of my love!

130-131 'If I'm faking, let the gods above punish me for cheapening my love!'

beguiled = put upon

OLIVIA   Ay me, detested! How am I beguiled!

VIOLA   Who does beguile you? Who does do you wrong?

OLIVIA   Hast thou forgot thyself? Is it so long?
    Call forth the holy father.

holy father = priest

Act 5, Scene 1

I told them they got married too quickly. I expect they want a divorce now.

Exit an Attendant

ORSINO   Come, away!   135

OLIVIA Whither, my lord? Cesario, husband, stay!

ORSINO Husband?

OLIVIA   Ay, husband. Can he that deny?

ORSINO Her husband, sirrah?

VIOLA   No, my lord, not I.

OLIVIA Alas, it is the baseness of thy fear

---

strangle thy propriety = hide your identity

139-143 *'You're afraid to say what you've done in front of Orsino. Don't be afraid. Admit it and you'll have no need to be afraid — being married to me makes you his equal.'*

That makes thee strangle thy propriety.   140
Fear not, Cesario, take thy fortunes up,
Be that thou know'st thou art, and then thou art
As great as that thou fear'st.

Enter PRIEST
                    O welcome, father!

144-148 *'You'd better explain what Cesario and I have done — even though we planned to keep it a secret.'*

Father, I charge thee by thy reverence
Here to unfold — though lately we intended   145
To keep in darkness what occasion now
Reveals before 'tis ripe — what thou dost know
Hath newly passed between this youth and me.

PRIEST A contract of eternal bond of love,

---

mutual joinder = joining

attested = proved

compact = promise

154 *'It's all proper because I'm a priest and I say it's true.'*

Confirmed by mutual joinder of your hands,   150
Attested by the holy close of lips,
Strengthened by th' interchangement of your rings,
And all the ceremony of this compact
Sealed in my function, by my testimony;
Since when, my watch hath told me, toward my grave   155
I have travelled but two hours.

157-160 *'You lying cub! What will you be like when you're grey-haired? Or will you get so cunning that your own tricks ruin you.'*

ORSINO *(To Viola)* O, thou dissembling cub! What wilt thou be
When time hath sowed a grizzle on thy case?
Or will not else thy craft so quickly grow
That thine own trip shall be thine overthrow?   160
Farewell, and take her, but direct thy feet
Where thou and I henceforth may never meet.

VIOLA My lord, I do protest —

OLIVIA   O, do not swear!
Hold little faith, though thou hast too much fear.

Enter SIR ANDREW *(his head bleeding)*

SIR ANDREW For the love of God, a surgeon! Send one   165

Rats!

presently = now

bloody coxcomb = bleeding head

170 *'I'd give £40 to be at home.'*

---

presently to Sir Toby.

OLIVIA What's the matter?

SIR ANDREW H'as broke my head across, and has given Sir
Toby a bloody coxcomb, too. For the love of God, your
help! I had rather than forty pound I were at home.   170

OLIVIA Who has done this, Sir Andrew?

SIR ANDREW The count's gentleman, one Cesario. We took
him for a coward, but he's the very devil incardinate.

ORSINO My gentleman Cesario?

---

the very devil incardinate = the devil himself

Od's lifelings = By God!

175-176 *'You cracked my skull for no reason. I only did what I did because Sir Toby put me up to it.'*

SIR ANDREW Od's lifelings, here he is! You broke my head for   175
nothing, and that that I did, I was set on to do't by Sir Toby.

VIOLA   Why do you speak to me? I never hurt you.
You drew your sword upon me without cause,
But I bespake you fair, and hurt you not.

bespake you fair =
spoke to you in friendly way

Enter SIR TOBY *and* FESTE

SIR ANDREW   If a bloody coxcomb be a hurt, you have hurt   180
me; I think you set nothing by a bloody coxcomb. Here
comes Sir Toby halting — you shall hear more; but if he had
not been in drink, he would have tickled you othergates than
he did.

halting = limping

182-184 'if Sir Toby hadn't been drunk
he would have given you a real hiding.'

ORSINO   How now, gentleman? How is't with you?   185

SIR TOBY   That's all one. H'as hurt me, and there's th' end on't.
Sot, didst see Dick surgeon, sot?

186 'He's hurt me, and
that's the end of it.'

sot = old drunk

FESTE   O, he's drunk, Sir Toby, an hour agone; his eyes were set
at eight i' th' morning.

188-189 'He was dead drunk
by eight this morning.'

SIR TOBY   Then he's a rogue, and a passy-measures pavin.   190
I hate a drunken rogue.

passy-measures pavin =
a slow, swaying dance

OLIVIA   Away with him! Who hath made this havoc with them?

SIR ANDREW   I'll help you, Sir Toby, because we'll be dressed
together.

dressed = bandaged

SIR TOBY   Will you help? — an ass-head, and a coxcomb,   195
and a knave, a thin-faced knave, a gull?

gull = fool

I've got a cock's comb too.

Show-off.

OLIVIA   Get him to bed, and let his hurt be looked to.

Exeunt FESTE, FABIAN, SIR TOBY, *and* SIR ANDREW

Enter SEBASTIAN

SEBASTIAN   I am sorry, madam, I have hurt your kinsman.
But had it been the brother of my blood,
I must have done no less with wit and safety.   200
You throw a strange regard upon me, and by that
I do perceive it hath offended you.
Pardon me, sweet one, even for the vows
We made each other but so late ago.

199-200 'Even if he'd been my
own brother, it would have been
the sensible and safe thing to do.'

ORSINO   One face, one voice, one habit, and two persons —   205
A natural perspective, that is and is not!

205-206 'The same face, voice
and clothes, but on two people.
It's a real-life illusion — true
and false at the same time!'

natural perspective = mirror
which makes double reflections

SEBASTIAN   Antonio! O, my dear Antonio,
How have the hours racked and tortured me,
Since I have lost thee!

ANTONIO   Sebastian are you?

SEBASTIAN   Fear'st thou that, Antonio?   210

ANTONIO   How have you made division of yourself?
An apple cleft in two is not more twin
Than these two creatures. Which is Sebastian?

211-213 'How have you split yourself
in two? These two look more alike
than the halves of an apple.'

OLIVIA   Most wonderful!

SEBASTIAN   Do I stand there? I never had a brother;   215
Nor can there be that deity in my nature
Of here and everywhere. I had a sister,
Whom the blind waves and surges have devoured.
Of charity, what kin are you to me?
What countryman? What name? What parentage?   220

216-217 'I haven't got magical
powers to be in two places at once.'

of charity = for pity's sake

VIOLA   Of Messaline. Sebastian was my father;

Act 5, Scene 1

Such a Sebastian was my brother, too;
So went he suited to his watery tomb.
If spirits can assume both form and suit,
You come to fright us.

suited = dressed

224-225 'If ghosts can have a body and clothes, then you've come to frighten us.'

SEBASTIAN   A spirit I am indeed,   225
But am in that dimension grossly clad
Which from the womb I did participate.
Were you a woman — as the rest goes even —
I should my tears let fall upon your cheek,
And say, 'Thrice welcome, drownèd Viola.'   230

225-227 'I am a sort of spirit, but still housed in the solid body I was born in.'

Now I'm confused.

VIOLA My father had a mole upon his brow.

SEBASTIAN   And so had mine.

VIOLA And died that day when Viola from her birth
Had numbered thirteen years.

233-234 'He died on Viola's thirteenth birthday.'

SEBASTIAN   O, that record is lively in my soul!   235
He finishèd indeed his mortal act
That day that made my sister thirteen years.

235-237 'I remember it well. He did die on my sister's thirteenth birthday.'

VIOLA If nothing lets to make us happy both,
But this my masculine usurped attire,
Do not embrace me, till each circumstance,   240
Of place, time, fortune, do cohere and jump
That I am Viola, which to confirm
I'll bring you to a captain in this town,
Where lie my maiden weeds; by whose gentle help
I was preserved — to serve this noble count.   245
All the occurrence of my fortune since
Hath been between this lady and this lord.

238-242 'If the only thing to stop us being happy is these men's clothes, wait till everything proves I'm Viola before you hug me.'

do cohere and jump = makes sense and agrees

maiden weeds = girl's clothes

246-247 'Everything that's happened to me since, has had to do with this lady and this lord.'

SEBASTIAN (To Olivia) So comes it, lady, you have been mistook.
But nature to her bias drew in that.
You would have been contracted to a maid —   250
Nor are you therein, by my life, deceived —
You are betrothed both to a maid and man.

248-249 'It turns out you've made a mistake. But nature made sure you would.'

contracted to a maid = engaged to a girl, i.e. Viola

maid = virgin, i.e. Sebastian

ORSINO Be not amazed, right noble is his blood.
If this be so — as yet the glass seems true —
I shall have share in this most happy wreck.   255
(To Viola) Boy, thou hast said to me a thousand times
Thou never shouldst love woman like to me.

253-255 'Don't be upset, he's got noble blood. If all this is really true, I'll have a share of this happy accident.'

VIOLA And all those sayings will I over-swear,
And all those swearings keep as true in soul
As doth that orbèd continent the fire   260
That severs day from night.

258-261 'Everything I've said, I'll say again. I'll keep my oaths as pure as the fire of the Sun.'

ORSINO   Give me thy hand,
And let me see thee in thy woman's weeds.

VIOLA The captain that did bring me first on shore
Hath my maid's garments — he upon some action
Is now in durance, at Malvolio's suit,   265
A gentleman and follower of my lady's.

263-266 'The Captain who brought me to shore has my girl's clothes. Now he's in prison — he's being sued by Malvolio.'

OLIVIA He shall enlarge him — fetch Malvolio hither.
And yet, alas, now I remember me,
They say, poor gentleman, he's much distract.

enlarge him = let him go

much distract = gone completely potty

                    Enter FESTE, with a letter, and FABIAN

A most extracting frenzy of mine own   270
From my remembrance clearly banished his.
How does he, sirrah?

270-272 'I was feeling quite mad myself, and it made me forget about Malvolio.'

FESTE   Truly, madam, he holds Belzebub at the stave's end as
well as a man in his case may do; h'as here writ a letter to
you — I should have given't you today morning. But as a   275
madman's epistles are no gospels, so it skills not much when
they are delivered.

273-274 'Madam, he's holding back the devil as best he can.'

275-277 'A madman's letters aren't gospel-truth, so it doesn't matter when they're delivered.'

OLIVIA   Open't and read it.

FESTE   Look then to be well edified when the fool delivers the
madman. *(Reads madly)* 'By the Lord, madam —'   280

279-280 'You're sure to learn a lot when a fool speaks for a madman.'

OLIVIA   How now, art thou mad?

FESTE   No, madam, I do but read madness — and your ladyship
will have it as it ought to be, you must allow *vox*.

283 'let me read it in character'

OLIVIA   Prithee read i' thy right wits.

285 'but to read it properly, you have to read it like a madman'

FESTE   So I do, madonna; but to read his right wits is to read thus. 285
Therefore, perpend, my princess, and give ear.

perpend: sort of means pay attention — but it's not a real word

OLIVIA   *(To Fabian)* Read it you, sirrah.

FABIAN   *(Reads)* 'By the Lord, madam, you wrong me, and the
world shall know it. Though you have put me into darkness,
and given your drunken cousin rule over me, yet have I the   290
benefit of my senses as well as your ladyship. I have your
own letter that induced me to the semblance I put on — with
the which I doubt not but to do myself much right, or you
much shame. Think of me as you please. I leave my duty a
little unthought of and speak out of my injury.   295
                              The madly used Malvolio.'

290-292 'I'm in my right mind as much as you are. I've got your letter, which told me to put on the appearance that I did.'

He's maaad!

OLIVIA   Did he write this?

FESTE   Ay, madam.

ORSINO   This savours not much of distraction.

299 'That doesn't sound very mad.'

OLIVIA   See him delivered, Fabian — bring him hither.   300

delivered = released

                    Exit FABIAN

My lord, so please you, these things further thought on,
To think me as well a sister, as a wife,
One day shall crown th' alliance on't, so please you,
Here at my house, and at my proper cost.

301-304 'Orsino, if you can think of me as a sister instead of a wife, we could celebrate our weddings together, at my house — and I'll pay.'

ORSINO   Madam, I am most apt t' embrace your offer.   305
(To Viola) Your master quits you — and for your service
                              done him,

305 'I'm delighted to accept your offer.'

quits = releases

So much against the mettle of your sex,
So far beneath your soft and tender breeding,
And since you called me master for so long,
Here is my hand — you shall from this time be   310
Your master's mistress.

mettle = nature

OLIVIA   A sister! You are she.

           Enter FABIAN *with* MALVOLIO

ORSINO   Is this the madman?

OLIVIA   Ay, my lord, this same.
How now, Malvolio?

Act 5, Scene 1

58

notorious = terrible

peruse = read

hand = handwriting

invention = writing style

316-323 'The letter is obviously written by you, so why did you give me such clear signals that you liked me? Why did you tell me to put on yellow stockings?'

lighter people = servants

suffered = allowed

geck and gull = twit and twerp

invention = trick

330-332 'It looks like my handwriting, but it's definitely Maria's.'

cam'st = you came

presupposed upon thee = suggested to you

337-340 'The trick worked really well on you, but when we know who thought it up, and why, you can defend yourself, and judge them.'

341-347 'I don't want the moment ruined with quarrels, so I'll admit that Toby and I set up the trick, after Malvolio was stubborn and rude.'

importance = insistence

recompense = repayment

350-353 'If you knew the wrongs on both sides you'd laugh at the trick.'

baffled thee = made a mockery of you

interlude = episode

but that's all one = but, who cares?

barren rascal = unfunny fool

360-361 'Time passes like a spinning top, and brings revenge.'

MALVOLIO   Madam, you have done me wrong,
Notorious wrong.

OLIVIA   Have I, Malvolio? No.

MALVOLIO Lady, you have. Pray you, peruse that letter.   315
You must not now deny it is your hand —
Write from it, if you can, in hand, or phrase,
Or say 'tis not your seal, not your invention.
You can say none of this. Well, grant it then,
And tell me, in the modesty of honour,   320
Why you have given me such clear lights of favour,
Bade me come smiling and cross-gartered to you,
To put on yellow stockings, and to frown
Upon Sir Toby, and the lighter people —
And acting this in an obedient hope,   325
Why have you suffered me to be imprisoned,
Kept in a dark house, visited by the priest,
And made the most notorious geck and gull,
That e'er invention played on? Tell me, why?

OLIVIA Alas, Malvolio, this is not my writing,   330
Though I confess much like the character.
But, out of question, 'tis Maria's hand.
And now I do bethink me, it was she
First told me thou wast mad — then cam'st in smiling,
And in such forms which here were presupposed   335
Upon thee in the letter. Prithee, be content —
This practice hath most shrewdly passed upon thee —
But when we know the grounds, and authors of it,
Thou shalt be both the plaintiff and the judge
Of thine own cause.

FABIAN   Good madam, hear me speak,   340
And let no quarrel, nor no brawl to come,
Taint the condition of this present hour,
Which I have wondered at. In hope it shall not,
Most freely I confess, myself and Toby
Set this device against Malvolio here,   345
Upon some stubborn and uncourteous parts
We had conceived against him. Maria writ
The letter, at Sir Toby's great importance,
In recompense whereof he hath married her.
How with a sportful malice it was followed   350
May rather pluck on laughter than revenge,
If that the injuries be justly weighed,
That have on both sides passed.

OLIVIA Alas, poor fool, how have they baffled thee!

FESTE Why, 'Some are born great, some achieve greatness, and   355
some have greatness thrown upon them.' I was one, sir, in
this interlude, one Sir Topas, sir — but that's all one. 'By the
Lord, fool, I am not mad.' But do you remember — 'Madam,
why laugh you at such a barren rascal, and you smile not,
he's gagged'? And thus the whirligig of time brings in his   360
revenges.

MALVOLIO I'll be revenged on the whole pack of you!

Exit

OLIVIA   He hath been most notoriously abused. ←

ORSINO   Pursue him, and entreat him to a peace. 365
He hath not told us of the captain yet.

Exit FABIAN

When that is known, and golden time convents, ←
A solemn combination shall be made
Of our dear souls. Meantime, sweet sister,
We will not part from hence. Cesario, come — 370
For so you shall be while you are a man,
But when in other habits you are seen,
Orsino's mistress, and his fancy's queen.

Exeunt (all but FESTE)

FESTE *(Sings)*
When that I was and a little tiny boy,
   With hey, ho, the wind and the rain,
A foolish thing was but a toy, 375
   For the rain it raineth every day.

But when I came to man's estate, ←
   With hey, ho, the wind and the rain,
'Gainst knaves and thieves men shut their gate, ←
   For the rain it raineth every day. 380

But when I came, alas, to wive,
   With hey, ho, the wind and the rain,
By swaggering could I never thrive,
   For the rain it raineth every day.

But when I came unto my beds, 385
   With hey, ho, the wind and the rain,
With tosspots still 'had drunken heads, ←
   For the rain it raineth every day.

A great while ago the world begun,
   With hey, ho, the wind and the rain, 390
But that's all one, our play is done,
   And we'll strive to please you every day.

Exit

363 'He's been treated incredibly badly.'

entreat him to a peace
= beg him to make peace

365-368 'When we have heard about the captain, and golden time brings us together, our souls will be joined in marriage.'

habits = clothes

fancy = love

375 'Foolish behaviour was just a game.'

Just me left, then.

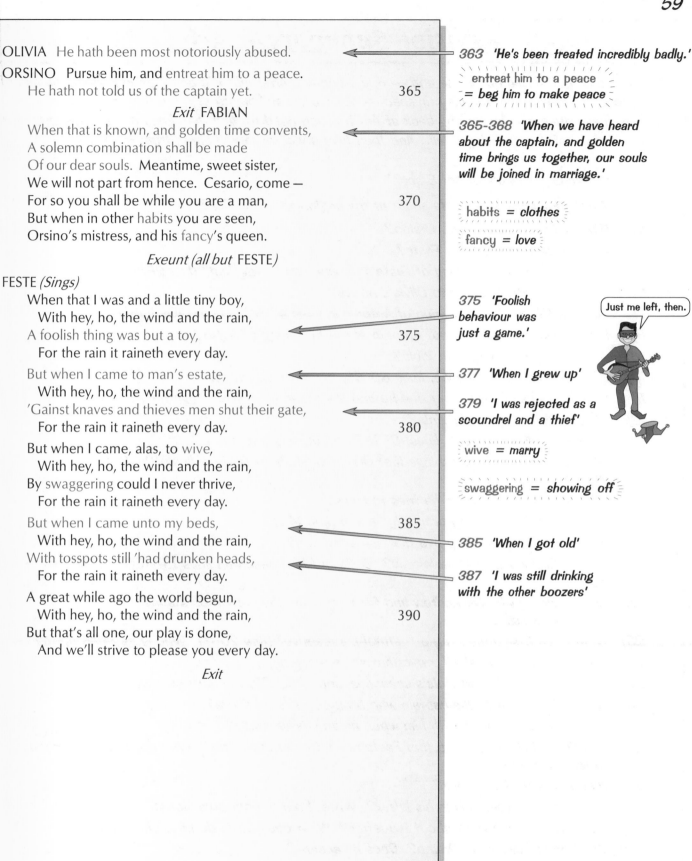

377 'When I grew up'

379 'I was rejected as a scoundrel and a thief'

wive = marry

swaggering = showing off

385 'When I got old'

387 'I was still drinking with the other boozers'

Revision Summary — Act 5

I knew it'd all get sorted out in the end — it is a comedy after all. It'd be no good if everyone ended up miserable. Well, that's the play finished — but there's still plenty of fun left in this book. Answer these questions by looking back at Act 5 if you need to, and then keep doing them until you don't need to refer to the play at all. And then take a well-deserved break from the Bard.

1) Where is the whole of Act 5 set?

2) What's Fabian asking Feste about at the beginning of the Act?

3) Who arrives on stage with Orsino?

4) What does Orsino give to Feste?

5) What's the double meaning of Feste's phrase "double-dealing" (line 25)?

6) Why does Antonio come to Olivia's house?

7) Write out Orsino's description of Antonio in lines 47-52 in your own words.

8) What does Viola think about Antonio at the beginning of Act 5?

9) Why is Antonio angry with Viola?

10) Write out Antonio's speech, lines 65-85, in your own words.

11) How long does Antonio say that he and Sebastian have spent together?

12) Why is Olivia angry with Viola?

13) Write out Olivia's speech, lines 101-103, in your own words.

14) Write out three insulting things that Orsino says about Olivia in lines 105-124.
    Why is he angry with her?

15) Who follows Orsino when he tries to leave?

16) What does "strangle thy propriety" mean (line 140)?

17) Who does Olivia ask to prove that she's married?

18) Why is Orsino angry at Viola now? Write out his speech on lines 157-160 in your own words.

19) What's wrong with Sir Andrew and Sir Toby when they arrive on stage?
    Who's responsible?

20) What does Orsino mean by a "natural perspective" (line 206)? Who is he referring to?

21) How does Viola say she'll prove that she's really a girl?

22) Write out Orsino's and Viola's speeches, lines 256-262, in your own words.

23) What's happened to the captain who brought Viola on shore?

24) What does Feste bring with him when he arrives on stage?

25) What's odd about the way that Feste reads the letter at first? Why does he say he has to read it like that?

26) Who reads the letter next?

27) What does Malvolio say in his letter? Write it out in your own words.

28) What does Orsino think about the letter? What does Olivia do after she hears it?

29) What does Olivia offer Orsino? Does he accept?

30) Who confesses to the trick on Malvolio?

31) When Malvolio finds out about the trick, would you describe him as:
    a) bitter and thirsting for revenge,   b) clinically insane
    or c) highly amused and likely to offer to buy everyone a drink?

32) Who does Orsino send to try to calm Malvolio down?

33) Who's the only person left on stage at the end of the play?